The Air Traveler's Survival Guide

The Plane Truth From 35,000 Feet

A. Frank Steward

D0963656

IMPACT PUBLICATIONS
Manassas Park, VA

Library of Congress Cataloguing-in-Publication Data

Steward, A. Frank
    The air traveler's survival guide: the plane truth from 35,000 feet / A. Frank Steward
        p. cm.
    ISBN 1-57023-171-0
    1. Air Travel – Anecdotes. 2. Air travel – Humor. 3. Steward, A. Frank. I. Title.

G151.S74 2001
387.7 – dc21   2001039389

Publisher: For information on Impact Publications, including current and forthcoming publications, authors, press kits, online bookstore, and submissions, visit our website: *www.impactpublications.com*

Publicity/Rights: For information on publicity, author interviews, and subsidiary rights, contact Media Relations Department: Tel. 703-361-7300, Fax 703-335-9486, or email: *info@impactpublications.com.*

Sales/Distribution: All bookstore sales are handled through Impact's trade distributor: National Book Network, 15200 NBN Way, Blue Ridge Summit, PA 17214, Tel. 1-800-462-6420. All other sales and distribution inquiries should be directed to the publisher: Sales Department, IMPACT PUBLICATIONS, 9104 Manassas Drive, Suite N, Manassas Park, VA 20111-5211, Tel. 703-361-7300, Fax 703-335-9486, or email: *info@impactpublications.com*

Contents

This is dedicated to the people who smile and thank you for your trash day in and day out.

Acknowledgments

I WANT TO THANK the whole Steward family – my wife Martha for her love and encouragement, my mother for my existence and her ability to be both parent and friend, my sister for her special help with the manuscript, and my brother for helping develop www.franksteward.com. I also want to thank everyone at Impact Publications for making this dream a reality. A special thank you to Mardie Younglof for her hard work and assistance. I would also like to thank Bob Joseph, Wendy Cohen, and Evelyn Metzger. And finally, I would like to thank you, the passengers and crews, for without you, the flying world would just be 'plane.'

Preface

LIFE IS A JOURNEY, not a destination. Always remember that it's the journey that is the true joy.

My objective in writing this book is not to offend, criticize, praise, or promote any persons, airlines, or aspect of the flying industry. My intentions are merely to share some observations, which in the past 13 years I have accumulated as a flight attendant. I may help you with future travel plans. Perhaps I can enlighten you about many of the different facets of flying, and the people who work on or sit around you in the airplane. All of that would be a bonus, for the main intention is to entertain you, to make you think, laugh, and compare the next time you fly.

Warning: The ability to laugh at yourself is strongly recommended.

If you have any comments about this book (good or bad), flying questions or stories to tell, visit my new online travel community at www.franksteward.com . . . and be frank!

1

Things That Go Bump in the Flight

Why On Earth...?

WHY IS IT THAT approximately 40% of all F/As (flight attendants) have a fear of heights?

Why would a profession that has so many beautiful women working in it attract predominantly gay men?

If peanuts are proven to produce gas, then why do F/As serve them eight miles in the air, in a plane with hundreds of people confined to one space, sitting next to each other?

Why are there ashtrays in the airplane toilets if you're not allowed to smoke in there (or anywhere on the plane for that matter) at any time?

Why is it that people wait until the seatbelt sign is turned on, or the meal service begins, to get up and use the toilet?

Why do all airlines always show the highest attended movies? If a hundred million people have seen Batman the Movie, don't you think most of the passengers would have also?

Why is it that after sitting down most of the time on a 14-hour flight, the first thing you want to do after you deplane is sit down?

Why does being in an airplane spark up an unusual thirst for ginger ale?

Why is it that you remember that you vowed never to fly a certain airline again halfway through their service?

Why do people wait until they get on an airplane to use the restrooms? Airports are pretty sophisticated these days. They offer big roomy stalls, nice sized sinks, and have many other features. Why would anyone choose a three-foot by three-foot cubicle over that? Nevertheless, the first thing most people do after finding their seat is head for the toilets.

Why are people suddenly allergic to fish when it's the only entree left?

Don't you think it's funny that no matter how bad the flight was, or how late you arrived, when the flight attendant reads the farewell from the airline they still read the same one? "We hope that you have enjoyed your flight with us and look forward to seeing you again on one of our flights." They should have an alternate in case of a bad flight: "We hope that your flight wasn't too bad and apologize for any inconveniences."

If laptop computers are issued by businesses to employees so they can work on the plane, why do most of them spend the entire flight playing "Doom," "Golf," or "Solitaire"?

Why is it that turbulence only seems to start when the F/As are in the middle of a coffee or meal service? I always wonder if the cockpit does it on purpose.

Why are there so many luggage stores at airports? You would think that the passengers about to board a flight would have their luggage needs covered by then.

If we can give you meals that cause indigestion and heartburn, why aren't we allowed to give out the cure, like Alka-Seltzer or Rolaids?

Why is the section of the airport from which the plane arrives and departs called a "terminal"? I refuse to eat in any place called the "Terminal Food Court."

Why do "direct flights" usually stop in a different city first? Doesn't sound very direct to me. The key phrase to listen for is the "nonstop flight."

Hmmm, just some things to think about.

Rats in the Belfry

THERE ARE ALWAYS STORIES of stowaway cats that circle the globe, or the dog that escapes when transiting the Fiji Islands. My story is of a different animal – a rat. Many Pan Am F/As knew him as Rodney the Rat. When Pan Am was still flying, they had different names for every aircraft painted on the nose, such as Clipper Mermaid, China Clipper, and Clipper Empress of the Sea. Rodney lived aboard Clipper Unity. To be more specific, he lived in First Class. There had been more than 50 reported sightings of Rodney worldwide, and numerous reports of him in the maintenance logbook.

The F/As thought that was a funny thing, but the Maintenance Department didn't share the same jubilation. The situation made the mechanics a laughingstock. They were furious, and determined to mount Rodney's head on a plaque.

The legend of this rodent was one of those stories that you hear about, but never actually believe – stories that others just talk about to keep the flight more interesting. Apparently, the mechanics had taken apart the whole section directly underneath the First Class cabin. They found his home, along with some sensitive wires that he had bitten through, but they never found Rodney. He had a hole in the cabin panel that they kept plugging up, but he just kept gnawing through.

I worked on Clipper Unity several times, but was never senior enough to work up front. I checked the logbook and verified that many documented reports had been made on Rodney. One day I heard that he was officially dead – pesticide had been his undoing Personally, I preferred to look at his demise as old age, or as too much to eat; I was sure that he died with a smile on his face.

Whatever the case, Rodney was no more; the sightings ceased, and he faded from everyone's memory.

I was pass-riding (flying as a standby passenger) to New York one day in October. The flight was fairly full, but I was able to get one of the last seats in First Class. I recognized the woman sitting across the aisle from me; she was the captain's wife and often flew on his flights. I settled in for a nice meal and an excessive amount of delicious and expensive red wine, then fell fast asleep.

Awaking midway through the flight, I spied the face of the captain's wife full of horror. It was as if she was screaming silently. It was dark in the cabin, so I couldn't make out right away why she was freaking out. Frozen with fear, she pointed at the First Class credenza (table). I saw nothing at first; but after a second glance, I made out a small puppy-like creature standing on its hind legs, attempting to grab a roll. I couldn't believe my eyes. It was Rodney! It had to be!

I just sat still staring at this legendary creature. He was brown and did not appear to have missed many meals. Two large teeth poked out of his mouth, but he was cute, in a strange sort of way. It was like meeting the movie star you always dreamed of meeting.

Everyone else was fast asleep. Everyone, that is, except the captain's wife, who by this time was close to passing out. Rodney looked around a bit, then settled on a half-eaten roll he found on the floor. I could tell he had his eyes on a specific pastry but it was out of his reach. With a roll wedged in his mouth he waddled toward the front of the cabin and disappeared through a hole between the wall panels, forcing the piece of bread through first.

The captain's wife shot out of her seat in an instant, and just as quickly, the captain came down to investigate the scene. I never in my life have seen a pilot react quicker. After checking the hole, he came over and asked if I had seen the rodent as well.

I smiled, nodded, and asked him, "What's the name of this airplane?"

"Clipper Unity, why?" he asked.

"Oh, no reason." I smiled like a little boy.

"You've heard of him too?" he inquired.

I nodded my head, and he continued, "I thought we got rid of him." He left for the cockpit, undoubtedly to write up another report. His wife, not surprisingly, never returned to her seat.

We landed in New York a few hours later. I waited until every First Class passenger had disembarked, then walked over to the hole that Rodney had disappeared through. I dropped the pastry he had been eyeing, and wedged it through with my foot.

Now that Pan Am has since gone out of business, I'm sure Rodney has retired to Florida somewhere and is probably bragging about his adventures in flight.

The Private Eye

YOU ARE ON AN extremely full and unbearably long flight. It doesn't have to be as boring as you think. Something I always do is play the "lookfer" game. Try and spot some of the funnier aspects and characters on a flight. Here is a short list to get you started:

At departures, look for the expression of extreme relief on the face of the husband, as his mother-in-law waves goodbye and steps onto the plane.

While boarding, look for the passenger who pretends to be asleep stretched across three seats, in order to reserve his bed.

How about the passengers who get on at the last minute with eight carry-on bags, and there's no luggage room left on the plane?

During take-off, watch out for the tough guys who forgot to tell their girlfriends about their fear of flying.

Inflight, look for the passenger who forgets about the pillow that's horse-shoed around his neck.

What about the man fast asleep whose head has turned, but his toupee hasn't?

The sweet F/A who just woke from her break...not so pretty and cheerful anymore.

The passenger fast asleep with his or her mouth so wide open that it makes you want to toss something into it.

The looks other passengers give the parents of a nearby crying baby.

The F/As who are so nice to a passenger, when you know that murder is on their mind.

How about the passengers who shout to each other with their earphones on?

Or the man who snores so loudly that you can feel it two cabins back.

Then there are the passengers who try to get out of their seats with their seatbelts or earphones still on.

The mother who didn't bring extra diapers or baby food.

The father who sits in First Class and occasionally visits his wife and kids in Economy.

Look behind you during the saddest part of a movie and see the hundreds of teary eyes.

The slumbering passengers forced to wake up by their seat partner for a mere apple or hot towel service.

The passengers who get into debates about how much time is left on the flight.

Look for the unfortunate passenger telling a gay joke to the wrong male F/A.

Watch the teetotalers order a double Scotch "unopened" when they discover booze is free. Then notice how much their carry-on bags begin to fill up with souvenirs.

Or the men who insist on going to the toilet during rough turbulence, and look for the result on their trouser legs.

Notice the lines for the toilets during rush hour, and watch the passenger at the back who may not be able to wait much longer.

What about the passenger who spends 20 minutes trying to pull the toilet door open, when it's clearly marked PUSH?

Or the face of the passenger when he discovers that he forgot his passport.

The passenger who practices aerobics in the back and is determined to walk around the plane for exercise...the 20th time you see him, you want him dead.

The commuting pilot who fights his way through all of the First Class passengers to be the first one off the plane.

Then there's that monotonous repetition, "buh bye, buh bye, buh bye," from the F/As as you leave.

Near Misses

OKAY, FIRST OF ALL, let's stop right there. There is no such thing as a near miss. If taken literally, a near miss is actually an impact. It's a term that is used way too much in the airline industry.

One of the most frequently asked questions is: "What was the worst, or scariest, incident that has ever happened to you on an airplane?" Compared to some of my flying partners, I have been rather lucky. I know people who were supposed to be on the flight that exploded over Lockerbie. A friend of mine was once sitting next to a man on an airplane who got sucked out into the engine during a rapid decompression (loss of cabin pressure). I fly frequently with a colleague who survived a ground collision between two 747s, where over 60 percent perished.

I have never (knock on wood) had anything that extreme happen to me, though I have been in situations which I wasn't sure I would survive. Some examples: A decompression where the wall panels were cracking five inches from me, exploding engines, pieces of wing falling off in-flight, landing gear not opening, radar malfunctions in the cockpit, fires onboard, bomb threats, turbulence so bad a fellow F/A hit the ceiling and broke her neck, to name a few.

Everyone has a certain story to tell about a flight on which they experienced their greatest fear. This is mine:

I was once a passenger traveling from Athens to Corfu on vacation. I was alone, because my girlfriend and I had broken up at the last minute, but I had decided to go on anyway. The wind was ferocious that night, but we still took off. If you have ever been on a Greek airline you know that everyone smokes, including the F/As. The bad turbulence had brought an extra thick cloud to the cabin air. We were bouncing around worse than I had ever experienced.

The flight attendants received a conference call from the cockpit and a worried expression grew on their faces. I knew that look – we were in trouble.

Smoke was bellowing out of one of the only two engines, and announcements were made over the speaker, but of course they were all in Greek. I knew it was bad news with all the screams and people reaching for lifejackets. The foreigners soon followed suit. The F/As were unable to prepare the cabin for an emergency landing because the turbulence was too extreme. Everyone was either putting away sharp jewelry, praying, or crying. There were even a few people who were writing quick notes to loved ones.

Oh my God! I was going to die in the Greek waters, or upon impact at Corfu. Morbidly, I wished that my ex-girlfriend was there to join me. People who didn't have their seatbelts fastened rolled down the aisles. We saw the island of Corfu and cheered, in between turbulent screams. How I yearned to be on that ground. I thought of the things in my life that I had and had not yet done. I had never been to a Greek island, although it seemed that that one would be my last. I was too young to die.

The pilot tried to land at an airfield before the airport, but the wind did not agree, so we forged on to the airport. I had the plane memorized, and decided which exit I would initially try for if I was conscious when we hit. I also instructed my seat partners around me to the proper bracing procedures for emergency landings. They didn't all speak English, but they copied my instructions nonetheless.

We circled the airport and spotted the six fire engines with the flashing lights there to greet us. The turbulence was so bad that while we were attempting to land, I could have sworn that we were upside down. I prayed like I had never prayed before. There was no way the plane could land in that position, but I guess the pilots had no choice. An unusual silence hit the air – a sort of terrified calm.

We were at a 90-degree angle, 50 feet from the ground, but miraculously, seconds before impact, the plane corrected and we hit landing gear first and bounced ten times, blowing all the tires before we were safe. Deafening cheers and applause rang throughout the cabin. Strangers hugged strangers; the older woman next to me dislodged her fingernails from my arm and kissed me.

We disembarked, and just about everyone, including myself, kissed the ground. I even had a cigarette though I wasn't much of a smoker, thinking that there were quicker ways to go. We danced on the runway; a few people broke out their bottles of duty-free ouzo, and we all drank a few hefty swallows. I was alone on a Greek island, had no hotel reservation, it was midnight – I had never been there before but, damn it, I was alive.

If you have a fear of flying, you are not alone. There are millions of fearful flyers out there. It may comfort you to know that air travel is the second safest mode of mass transportation in the world. Second only to the escalator and elevator.

There are programs designed for those who have this fear, but unless you have a severe case, I would recommend working this problem out with a loved one who is an experienced flyer. Those programs can get fairly expensive, and after you have conquered the fear of flying, you most probably will gain a fear of your next credit card bill. While on board, if you feel apprehensive, notify a flight attendant. We are there to reassure you as well.

She Couldn't Bare It

IT WAS EARLY SEPTEMBER, and the typical summer rush was almost over. I was flying back from Europe, dreaming of the days that every seat on the plane wasn't full. Unfortunately, this flight wasn't one of them. In fact, we had to fight for our crew rest seats. The flight was full and nearly void of any interesting characters, passengers or crew. There was one pretty young lady who did stand out. She had long curly blonde hair, no make-up, and dark circles under her eyes as if she had been crying. She didn't eat or drink anything. She just sat there in a daze with the blankest of expressions. My heart went out to her; I wanted to help, but could tell she wanted to be left alone.

I lost track of her throughout the flight until one of the F/As in the galley dropped his coffee.

"Oh my God!" he shrieked and pointed.

I looked up the aisle and couldn't believe my eyes. There was my sad young lady, walking back from the lavatory without a stitch of clothing. I could tell she was on the verge of tears. Some men cheered, and other passengers gasped. I went into automatic mode, grabbed the nearest blanket and wrapped it around her in a hug-like manner. She hugged me back and cried uncontrollably. I walked her into the crew rest area and closed the curtains. She cried for about 15 minutes, and I tried to calm her down.

She couldn't speak. I went to the elderly couple in the seats next to where she was sitting, but they didn't know her. They told me that she had said nothing the whole flight but disappeared to the toilet for the last 30 minutes. I inspected the toilet but found nothing. I looked into her purse in search of clues. Inside, I found some used tissues, keys, a crumpled-up note, and a half-bottle of vodka. I brought it back and tried talking to her, but she didn't reply. She merely pointed to the note for me to read. It was a note from her boyfriend saying that it was over, and he was getting back together with his wife and children.

"I have wasted the last five years of my life," she said softly. She fought back the convulsions that accompany heavy crying.

"I am sorry for your pain, but what did you do with your clothes and why?"

"I'm sorry to cause a scene. I just realized that he had bought me everything I was wearing. I stuffed everything down the toilet." She began to cry again.

I got my suitcase down and went through it for anything that might fit her. I handed her my college sweatshirt and a pair of blue jeans. She got dressed and looked quite good in my clothes. I found her sandals in the lavatory trash.

I talked to her for about an hour, and tried to console and sober her up.

"Am I going to get in trouble for this?" she asked.

"No, the crew and I feel that it wouldn't be for the best, but you do know that you need counseling, right?"

"Yes, I guess you may be right. I am so sorry and appreciate everything that you have done for me."

She fell asleep for the rest of the flight. When we arrived, she asked for my address in order to return my clothes. I gave it to her but never expected to get them back. Still sad and slightly embarrassed, she gave me a kiss on the cheek and walked away.

One year later, I received a package with three new university sweatshirts, a pair of blue jeans, and a wedding invitation. No, it wasn't to the married boyfriend but to her counselor.

Three years later, she sent me a letter with a family picture of herself and her husband with their twin boys. In the letter, she told me that she had found more happiness than she ever dreamed possible. They laugh together about how they met. She added, "I *barely* remember but will never forget."

It's fascinating that the road of life is never clear. One wrong turn could eventually lead you to the highway. I'm not suggesting that everyone take off their clothing during the flight. (The term "friendly

skies" would take on a whole new meaning.) However, I am propos-
ing that everyone embrace life's detours and be open to change. I met
my wife during a flight cancellation, and that was the best flight I
never took.

2

Anything But Plane People

Lost in the Translation

ACCENTS ARE WONDERFUL; they are the variables that make the English language interesting. They are the ingredients that seem to spice up this plain but popular way of talking.

I can pretend to be an accent expert, but have to admit that I am wrong more times than right. I have learned the hard way to ask, "Where do you come from?" rather than guessing the origin of an accent. People are generally very proud of their homeland, and might be offended if you guessed a rival country.

It could be a simple variation like Canadians placing an "eh" after most sentences. The Australian accent is a laid back pronunciation, and an 'O' is put directly behind many words – for example, "freo" and "righto." A Japanese accent often pronounces the "l's" as "r's," as in Honoruruu, instead of Honolulu. The Irish say their th's as straight t's. "Three hundred and thirty-three" would be pronounced "tree hundred and tirty-tree." In addition, some British would pronounce that "free hundred and firty-free."

It's the beauty of cultural diversity, and while you may say that they have a great accent, they are probably thinking the same about yours. Yes, believe it or not, everyone, even you, has an accent.

It's when a person has a different comprehension of a common saying that things can get interesting.

He was a small wide-eyed Indian man. His balding head was poorly disguised with the few long strands of hair combed over from one side to the opposite. His extremely thin body accented his facial features, with glasses about three sizes too big for his face. Never before had he ventured out of Bombay, and was obviously very excited about visiting America. The beaming smile never left his face.

He spoke no English except a few sentences that had obviously been taught to him at a previous date.

"I am begging your pardon, one walking Johnny, please," he asked with a smile and a round nod of the head.

"'Walking Johnny'?" I asked.

"Walking Johnny, walking Johnny," as he pointed to the tray of liquor miniatures in my cart.

"Ah, Johnny Walker Scotch." I gave it to him with a can of soda water just in case.

He nodded his head and replied, "From the heart of my bottom, I am thanking you."

I chuckled to myself and just thought he might have switched it by mistake this once. I soon discovered that this was one of the only English expressions that he knew, and was quite proud to say it with every gesture.

"From the heart of my bottom, I am thanking you."

Now, if I were to thank people from the heart of my bottom, I am sure that people would be offended. I think he was trying to say, "from the bottom of my heart," but there was no way we could convey to this man that this phrase was wrong. Although we had a fun time trying, I am sure he spent his American tour thanking people from the heart of his bottom.

I always wondered if a family member taught him this saying wrong on purpose, as a joke. It happens more than you think, and if you think about it, it's a pretty good joke. Therefore, I tried it.

A while back, I got lucky because I had a month of Stockholm trips. I was excited because I had never been to Sweden, and normally couldn't fly these trips, because I was too junior. I wanted to learn as much of the language as possible. On the first trip, I befriended the Swedish translator on board and asked her many questions regarding pronunciations and sayings. I probably massacred the language, but felt proud that I had tried.

The next trip, I flew with a new F/A named Jack. He, too, was excited because this was his first trip. He must have seen too many Swedish erotic films, because all he wanted to do was meet "Swedish babes" on his layover. He wanted to ask the translator some pick-up lines in Swedish, but was too shy because the translator was a woman. I told him that I would ask her later, but he kept pestering me until I asked.

I devised a plan. I asked the translator in confidence to tell me what "I have a very small penis" was in Swedish. She blushed but told me anyway. I memorized it, and told him that when he met a beautiful girl on his layover, he should tell her how beautiful she was by repeating the following line, "Jag har en liten snopp."

He repeated and memorized it the whole flight. He said it aloud a few times. I knew that he was saying it right when a Swedish passenger laughed as he overheard. The thought of him using the line for "potential babes" kept me in tears of laughter the whole layover.

A friend of mine tried the same thing in Italy, except this time he told the new F/A how to say "Nobody move, this is a stickup," instead of "I would like to exchange some money." Halfway through the line at the bank, they wisely decided to let him in on the joke.

We get languages onboard from Swahili to Lithuanian, and many times the passengers speak no more than one or two words of English. A lot of the time they will have a note written in English by their family, but it usually doesn't help when we ask them about their meal choices. In this case, we either give them the choice they would probably like (which is usually the one that we have more of), or we act out the dish. If it's chicken, we fold our arms under our shoulders and flap our wings. Alternately, if it's fish, we purse our lips and act like a fish, and so on. Degrading, isn't it? It gets more interesting when the meal choice is lasagna.

We were short of special meals one day, so I had to make sure that everyone who had a special meal had ordered one. I approached a Romanian woman sitting quietly by the window.

"Excuse me, are you passenger Patel?" I said with a hot vegetarian meal in my hand.

She lowered her tray table and said in a deep accent, "Yes, I am ungrey."

"No, ma'am, I realize that you're hungry, but I have to know if you ordered a special meal. Are you passenger Patel?" She obviously didn't understand me and didn't get the point of my question.

"No, I'm ungrey," she stood her ground and I stood mine.

"Yes, but is your name Patel?" I began to chuckle in frustration. We went back and forth for several minutes, until a woman tapped me on the shoulder and said, "I am passenger Patel, and that, is passenger Ungrey."

Oops!

A fellow F/A was attempting to assist a Nigerian woman in the back of the airplane with her Customs card. She spoke very little English, and surprisingly he was doing a good job. I came back to get some supplies and noticed a perplexed look on his face.

"What's wrong?" I asked.

"How do you say, 'Do you have any food items with you,' in Nigerian?"

Knowing that he really didn't expect me to know, I replied, "Ooobuh doobouh dabbaah gurumbullieah."

He looked at me, impressed, and thanked me, turned to the woman and repeated it perfectly, "Ooobuh doobouh dabbaah gurumbullieah."

The woman looked at him as if he was a madman and ran up the aisle in horror. I couldn't actually believe that he took me seriously. The woman was too afraid to talk with him again. He never lived that one down.

On a flight to Scotland, a male passenger approached the galley with a big wide grin and large red nose that would make Rudolph proud.

"Choloh mie wiftie felocher hercah deloo," he stated.

What language was that, I wondered, only to discover that it was English but with the heaviest Scottish accent that I had ever heard.

"What was that again?" I politely replied.

He nudged me as if he was telling a joke. "Ah kee mon, choloh mie wiftie felocher hercah deloo!" He smiled as if he just finished the punch line.

Now being an ex-bartender and realizing that when in doubt you should pretend to get the joke or they'll end up repeating it until you do, I gave him a laugh and a brush-off line.

"You've got that right. That's a good one." I patted him on the shoulder in a friendly manner and walked away.

Ten minutes later he re-appeared in the galley looking for me. This time his smile was strained and he had an expectant look on his face.

"Whatten ta due boot me wiftern?" he stated.

The gig was up. "I'm sorry, sir, I don't understand you. What are you telling me?"

"De Loo, De Loo, mie wifter die locher in De Loo!"

"Oh, the loo [English for toilet], it's around the side to the left."

The smile on his face diminished. "Ach laddy, you dunno understand."

At this point an elderly Scottish man in the galley spoke up. "I tank, young man, he's trying to tell you that his lady is locked in the toilet."

"Oh my gosh," I exclaimed as I ran to the lavatory.

The door had come off its hinges and wedged itself into the paneling. It took about ten minutes to get the door open. Meanwhile I heard several rounds of "ooh gooness me" coming from inside.

We opened the door and there stood a large lady who was the spitting female image of her husband with the same wide grin.

"I am terribly sorry, ma'am!" I prepared for a yelling.

"Chor ain look dat am nay American cos aid sooh. Nay maind, hoo boot a wee brandy tecall teven."

Translation: You're in luck that I am not American because I would sue. Never mind, how about a small brandy and we will call it even.

"My pleasure." She was such a good sport that I gave her the whole bottle of expensive cognac from First Class as a present. As the couple got off the plane on arrival, she thanked me and said what I can only guess to be " you can lock me in the toilet anytime if it gets me a gift like that." Mind you, that is only a guess.

The Human Race

WHO'S WINNING THIS RACE? Nobody. My feeling is that we're all losing, but that's not for me to say. The following is a generalization, a guide, and an attempt at enlightenment. It's not a rule, but a norms path for everybody (except Norm), to assist you in your travel with the various cultures and races that you might encounter. I do not in any way mean to offend anyone by wrong portrayal of culture or habits, and I am sorry if I do so here.

It seems that many people don't understand that there are many lifestyles, cultures, and traditions out there. More importantly, the person you're sitting next to might be offended by something that you're doing right now.

The Americans

I'll start with the Americans because, being one myself, and flying for an American carrier, I can speak with some authority on this matter. Americans can be very peculiar and sometimes the most frustrating passengers. So many haven't quite mastered the concept of what exactly the airline industry is all about. Air travel is a mode of transportation from A to B. It's not a day care center, gourmet restaurant, or a counseling service. While all these facets are sometimes available, the airline's primary purpose remains being a mode of transport.

Americans want as much as they can get. Three drinks at a time, special meals, cards, upgrades, empty seats next to them, and an ear to bend when everything isn't perfect. While I respect the urge to get the most in life, I equally respect the understanding that there are other people on the airplane, and on this earth, for that matter.

Unfortunately, the Americans are the only nationality as a whole who generally haven't mastered a second language, but the ones who do try are somewhat admired for it (except possibly in Paris).

On the other hand, Americans can be among the most friendly and outgoing people around. They are not afraid to look or act like tourists, and can spark up conversations with complete strangers. I can be on a flight to Europe and pick out Americans without hearing them speak. There is something about them that exudes friendliness and ignorance mixed into one.

The British

British passengers are an odd but interesting subject. When they are upset they seldom show it, and when they are pleased you very rarely know it. I had an elderly British couple on a flight, and could tell that they were obviously not happy. They hardly touched their meals, never smiled, talked, or watched the movie. They were upset and there was nothing I or anyone else could do about it. At the end of the flight they made it a point to approach me. I thought to myself, "Oh, here we go, time to yell at the F/A." They shook my hand, smiled and told me what a wonderful flight they'd had. It was their best flight ever.

The British often drink tea like it was water, and even though they might be the first to make fun of their monarchy, they are also the first to defend it. I am convinced that if there wasn't a monarchy in Britain, there would be 50% less newspapers in England. I haven't worked out the difference between the British and English yet, but not all British are English, and vice versa. Never make the mistake of saying that Irish, Scottish, and English are the same thing – it's a big insult; I found out the hard way.

One of the unique characteristics of the British is their nose-blowing technique. It seems to be somewhat of a sport over there. I was a passenger on a flight to London once, sitting next to this older man with bushy eyebrows in a pinstriped suit. He was, for a lack of better words, a very proper gentleman. He had a very drawn-out accent, and said a lot of "rahthers, Brahvohs," and all that. His demeanor was pleasant, and his manners were impeccable.

At one stage, he carefully and methodically unfolded a handkerchief. He raised it discreetly to his nose and let out the loudest honking noise, which startled me, to say the least. I thought that the English woman next to him would be appalled, but she didn't take the slightest bit of notice. A few minutes later she did the same, only louder. When three people in my cabin honked at once, I couldn't help but laugh. Of course, they all noticed that, and looked at me as if I was some kind of lunatic.

The Japanese

The Japanese, armed with their camcorders and loaded cameras, are often the easiest and most ideal passengers. I am amazed that anyone would want so many pictures of the inside of an airplane. They are very courteous and respectful of a F/A's job. There's hardly a complaint to be had, and they usually finish 99% of the food on their plate.

One downside to Asia flying is the smoking problem. The concept of not smoking while standing cannot be grasped. Now that all airlines are changing to a non-smoking policy, I guess everyone will have to learn.

A hint for people who don't have U.S. passports: if you are traveling to Hawaii from anywhere other than the U.S., try to be one of the first ones off of the plane, then hurry through Customs. With the number of Japanese visitors to Hawaii, the wait at Immigration can be very long. An old girlfriend of mine once took four and a half hours.

The French

The French know what they want and when and how they want it. No meal or wine served on an aircraft will meet their expectations, for they place a very high value on eating and drinking. Just as everything is bigger and better in Texas, so it is with the French. They believe that their wine is better, their cheese is the best, and their culinary expertise unrivaled in the world.

Very hard to please, they are usually fairly cordial, though they often carry a supercilious attitude with them wherever they go. No self-respecting Frenchman would do otherwise. It is as if he is saying, "Challenge me...I dare you."

The Indians

When one says the word "Indian," one might imagine a feather headdress and moccasins. I am referring, instead, to people from India. The women who might be wearing saris (long colorful dresses), and the men with turbans. I once worked a flight to Bombay and was briefed on certain techniques for an easier flight (considering that it was my first to India).

A vegetarian meal is almost a certainty, and confusion is never far away. When asked a yes or no question, a round nod of the head and a wave of the hand are replied. By a round nod, I mean a yes and no nod in one.

Sometimes body odor is a factor, because many Indian religions do not allow the use of alcohol in any form, which most antiperspirants include. Therefore, it is not a widely marketed item in India.

Don't shake hands or serve food with the right hand. In some places in India toilet paper is not an option, and the right hand is used to wash with. On the Bombay flight, an Indian woman unaware of the toiletry customs of the American-owned airline, exited the restroom with bright blue hands (the color of the toilet water). It was a most bizarre spectacle, until one of the F/As explained to me that some people were not used to wash basins, and that particular lady had washed her body with the toilet water. It apparently happened a lot on that route.

One final curious note: on that flight, where vegetarian meals are denoted by seat number and last name, there were 80 to 85 meals for passengers with the last name of Patel. It's apparently the most common name in India. The name Singh came in second with 30. A fellow crew member decided to prove it to me and made an announcement on the P.A. "Would a passenger Patel please ring their call button." I have never heard so many bells in my whole career. It makes you wonder what the phone book looks like.

The Australians and New Zealanders

I have learned through trial and error never to bunch Australians and New Zealanders together. Both countries have made it perfectly clear that each is a separate entity. In this section, however, I am combining the two countries.

The Aussies and the Kiwis are usually fun and enjoy their drinks. But, quite frankly, if you run into one on a flight, he has undoubtedly been traveling for many hours and would prefer to sleep through the flight.... unless it's a rugby or surfing group, which is a whole different chapter altogether.

I was working a half-full flight from Los Angeles to Frankfurt. That day many of our passengers were upset; before the flight, the gate had been changed three times. A young man got on and went straight to sleep. I didn't wake him because I could see by the tag on his bag that he had just connected from an Australia flight, and any sleep would probably be appreciated. Ten hours into the flight he stretched, opened his eyes to a nice hot breakfast, and looked around in horror.

"Breakfast? What time is it? When are we going to get there?" he asked in a confused panic.

"We arrive in Frankfurt in about two hours," I replied, thinking that he was probably in disbelief about how long he had slept.

"Frankfurt? I am going to San Francisco! This plane is going to San Francisco, isn't it?"

Oops. He was put on the first plane to San Francisco once we arrived in Frankfurt. The airline even upgraded him, realizing that technically he wasn't supposed to be able to get on the wrong flight with the new computerized seating plan. He was a good sport about it, remarking that he did think it was strange that they checked his passport before he got on a flight to San Francisco. I guess you could say that he took the longest one-hour flight ever.

The Germans

The Germans are here, and, boy, are they traveling up a storm. With the strength of their currency and the millions of new faces with the

East – West unification, tourism has exploded. Why pay more in your own country when you can pay less abroad. They enjoy their beers, and can be quite enjoyable passengers. Every flight should be catered with 90% beef selection, because not many Germans will pick the fish or vegetarian pasta selections.

They generally speak quite adequate English, although I can't tell you how many times I've heard this sentence, "You have a beer for me?" Which, incidentally, usually means three or four.

You know how the Germans always get credited with laying their towels out early at prime spots around hotel pools? Well, I even saw one older German man spread his towel across a row of empty seats on a flight. It was his way of reserving them, I guess. It worked.

The Jewish Passenger

One of the great concepts of flying is observing and respecting the various cultures that come your way. You might notice a man with a black top hat, long curls extending from his sideburns, and a fairly long beard. If his wife is traveling with him, she is very likely to be wearing a wig. Nine times out of ten, they are Jewish, or more properly known as Hasidic Jews.

They'll most likely have a kosher meal. Many of the men will pray during the flight, usually at sunset or sunrise. They will lay out a mat and do their procession quietly. Try not to stare, and never disturb them once they have started. While many would frown on their views towards women, they are usually fairly tame seat partners.

I was scheduled to work on a flight to Munich one September evening, when I got pulled off and rescheduled for a Tel Aviv flight. A Jewish group had specifically requested a male service, and on that particular flight there were none. I was delighted because I had never been there before, but the F/A who was pulled off was not amused. While I am no expert on the Jewish faith, I was told that it had to do with women and their monthly cycle.

When sundown was determined, half of the plane was standing, chanting, and praying. It was an unusual and interesting sight to see, but it made toilet access quite impossible.

On my return flight, I was in charge of a little boy six years old, who was flying by himself (known in airline terms as an "unaccompanied minor"). He was seated next to a very proud Hasidic Jewish man. The man called me over and insisted that the little boy be moved to another seat. He did not want to sit next to an "obviously spoiled non-Jewish brat." The boy had done nothing to deserve the unfair label. I did try to move him, though – not for the man's sake, but for the little boy's. However, it was a full flight and I was unable to reseat him.

The man decided to take it upon himself to try and educate the little boy on how bad his parents' religion was, and how the little boy lived a corrupted lifestyle, and so on. The little boy, not thrilled with insults about his parents, eventually fell asleep, and there was peace for the time being. Luckily, when the child woke up, the man had just fallen asleep.

Toward the end of the flight, I was serving breakfast at the front of the cabin and looked back on the boy to see if all was well. Out of the corner of my eye I saw him doing something rather curious. I couldn't quite make it out. He was standing on his seat and bending over the man with a pair of scissors. OH MY GOD! NO!

I wanted to yell out to him but everyone was sleeping. With one snip of the scissors, the right lock of the Jewish man's hair was severed. I ran back to prevent World War III. The boy just sat there with the biggest smile on his face, holding up the strand of hair and looking at it, as the man continued to slumber away.

I got the little boy's bags and moved him up to First Class in a hurry, for fear of what this man might do when he woke up. Imagine the amount of time it must have taken him to grow it and, more importantly, it was part of his religion. I put the lock of hair into the man's bag to avoid further embarrassment, and waited for the worst to happen.

We were on our final descent when the man finally woke up. A curious thing happened: he didn't notice the lock was missing. He was bound to discover his loss if he went to the restroom, but luckily he was too late for that, because the seatbelt sign was on. I hid from the man, but kept an eye on him just in case. We landed, and he deplaned without noticing. I didn't have the heart or the guts to tell him.

The boy stood at the door with the captain's hat on and waved a big smiling goodbye to the man when he got off. He merely waved back in disgust, and disappeared into the sea of people. I don't know if it was my imagination or not, but I could have sworn that I heard a yell of despair when I walked through the terminal. I walked a bit faster.

The Russians

The typical Russian passenger is very appreciative of everything, being accustomed to the misadventures of Aeroflot, the Russian airline. But, from experience on that airline, they don't trust checking in any baggage and thus will overload the overhead storage bins.

I had a wonderful three-day layover in Moscow. I drank vodka in the university district and did a lot of historical tours, but by the end of the three days I was ready to get back to more familiar surroundings. A friend from home had heard that I was going to Russia, and asked me to bring him back a military parachute watch. I was able to find one on the black market, and got one for myself as well.

At the Moscow airport there were the traditionally long lines at immigration and customs. I was the only one out of my crew that got sent to secondary screening, where they ask a few questions or go through your bags. I was told that one crew member always got searched. The inspector went through every inch of my bags and found the watches. He threw them down to the ground and stepped on them. He told me in a stern voice that I wasn't allowed to take military artifacts out of Russia. I didn't know – it was my first time there. He instructed me to put my hands on the wall and spread my legs.

One would have thought that I was smuggling drugs. It was embarrassing with passengers and crew looking on. Who would want to smuggle stupid military watches on their body?

I was a bit bewildered when I got on the plane, and was relieved when we finally took off. A portly man came to the back, looked out the window, and repeated what could only be described as Russian obscenities. He took off his coat and continued to take off no less than 18 identical military parachute watches. They were taped to various places on his body. He had seen my ordeal earlier, gave me one, and remarked, "Hot seller in Amuricah." I never gave it to my friend; I felt as if I had earned it. It stopped working three months later, anyway.

Scandinavians

You can expect a depleted liquor supply by the end of the flight, with alcohol being so expensive in the Scandinavian countries, though it is fair to say that they are masters at holding their liquor and seldom get loud or out of hand. I was on a flight to Stockholm when we ran out of every type of liquor on board – in the First, Business, and Economy classes. It's common to run out of beer and wine, but every miniature of liquor, as well?

You could never tell by walking through the cabin that this much drinking had taken place; everyone was calm and quite sober. An elderly man told me that it was bad planning on my airline's behalf. They should know to stock double the amount of alcohol for the Stockholm flights. I agreed. We broke the rules and decided to let them drink their own duty-free liquor if they wanted to do so.

Scottish

Aye, the Scottish passengers are among my favorites. They are usually cheerful and courteous, with a kind word and a ready smile or laugh. They enjoy their Scotch drinks, but seldom overdo it. I worked a flight to Scotland once, and never had so much fun in all of my ten years of flying. Many passengers were dressed up in old Scottish costumes, drinking out of tankards, and acting out roles. They were going over for the Edinburgh Renaissance Fair. They made sure they showed that a true Scot wears nothing under his kilt.

On that flight, nobody slept. It was my first time to Scotland, and there was no shortage of suggestions on how to spend my two-day layover. A couple of families even invited me to their homes to experience the real Scotland. We talked the night away. I was fascinated by their accents, but I have to admit I only understood about 60 percent of what they had said. It's not very often that I am disappointed when a flight ends.

South Americans

They love their hot chocolate, and if there is none, they have coffee with about seven or more sugars. A "pssst" or a click of their fingers is the way most get the attention of an F/A. Pleasant enough, they can get out of hand now and then. Many are not accustomed to such a big airplane. And that gorgeous 22-year old woman you're staring at? She could be no more than 12.

We were flying to Rio de Janeiro during the final of the World Cup soccer match. Brazil was in the final, so the captain made the soccer broadcast available on the airplane radio. Need I say it was the noisiest flight ever? When Brazil scored it was like a bomb had gone off in the cabin. When they won, everyone celebrated and danced the flight away. I am not just talking about the younger crowd; the old ladies cheered, too. Soccer, football as they call it, is serious business in Brazil. The celebration lasted for our entire layover. There were street parties, dancing, and fireworks. I didn't get much sleep, but talk about being in the right place, at the right time.

Open Mouth, Insert Foot

WE IN THE AIR also blunder from time to time. The following story is my biggest example. It was to be a wonderful flight: I was in love; it was spring; we had a light load and a great crew; and we were flying to Italy. All the factors of a great flight were there. The flight progressed as usual, the beverage and meal service, duty-free shopping, then the movies. It was time for the passengers to relax and perhaps sleep.

"PING," the call bell sounded from someone in Economy.

I was the closest, so I ventured up to the passenger. "Yes sir, what can I do for you?" I was in the best of spirits, so no amount of call bells could dampen them.

"Yes, could I please have a Coca-Cola?" A nice-looking young man asked.

"Certainly," I replied and returned with the request.

"I'm sorry, could I have that without ice?" he sheepishly requested.

"Sure, no problem." I complied.

Ten minutes later another "PING" sounded in the galley. It was him again. This time he wanted lemonade. Nothing could tarnish my good mood, but I was a bit curious as to why he found it necessary to ring his call bell for everything, especially since he was on the aisle, and the closest passenger to the galley. I got him his lemonade without ice, but that time he wanted ice. No less than five minutes elapsed before he rang it again, this time for some peanuts. I decided that it was time to drop this kind but call-button-sensitive gentleman a hint.

I returned with the peanuts. I smiled and pleasantly remarked,

"You know, we aren't so bad in the back. We have a bar all set up for any requests you might have, so feel free to get up and come visit us if you should need anything else. It would probably do you some good to stretch your legs anyway." I was quite proud of the way I had expressed it.

He motioned me closer and said in a low voice, "That sounds like a good idea, except for one thing." He removed the blanket from his lap and continued, "I don't have any legs."

Horrified and ashamed, I quietly whispered, "My God, I am deeply sorry." I wanted to curl up into a ball and disappear.

I should have listened in briefing and been more aware of his situation during boarding. But no, I was too busy making plans for Italy. I guess you could say that I didn't have a leg to stand on.

I stayed and talked with him a while. To be honest, I was initially only trying to work off my guilty feelings, but then I became intrigued by this young man's story.

"I'm going to backpack alone across Europe. My parents told me I couldn't, friends said I shouldn't, and everyone else claimed I wouldn't. I am 20, starting college in the fall, and have never been to Europe. So what if I take a little longer to board the train. With my wheelchair, I have always got a guaranteed seat."

I marveled at his tenacity, sense of adventure, but most of all his courage. If the roles were reversed, I am not certain that I could be as confident. I had a difficult enough time going to new countries alone, much less with a major disability.

The flight ended, and as usual there was no aisle wheelchair waiting for him at the airport. I put the makeshift one we had on the plane together and wheeled him to the front door. He loaded his customized backpack onto his wheelchair, turned, smiled, and rolled away.

Disability awareness in the airlines is getting better but still has a way to go. There are better facilities at airports, specially equipped lavatories on the airplane, Braille aircraft information cards, safety demonstration videos with captions, and telephones for passengers with hearing loss (amplified phones and text phones, commonly known as TTYs).

The flight attendants are trained to give special briefings to the disabled passenger about emergency procedures. Even if you are a seasoned traveler with a disability, we are still required to brief you. Make sure you let your F/A know of your special needs and requests. If you want to be left alone or treated like a regular passenger, tell them that as well. Bring a note, board early, pull us aside, do anything to convey the message and be specific. We can't respect your wishes until we know them.

Quite often I pass a F/A briefing, or a fellow passenger talking, very loudly if not shouting to a disabled traveler. The problem with that is if they are deaf, they may not hear you well or at all, and if they are blind, they generally have a keener sense of hearing and you're probably hurting their ears. It's kind of like when you don't know a foreign language so you speak English louder, slower, and with a silly accent. It does nothing to help the situation but sounds better in your mind.

Unfortunately, not too many flights are met at arrival with the correct amount of wheelchairs, and we end up waiting 30 minutes for proper assistance (many times resulting in misconnections). Then there are the instances when the jetway breaks down and the stairs are used instead. The airline is always at a loss on what to do about our wheelchair passengers. Shouldn't there be some set procedure planned for when this happens?

If you have a disability, when you call and confirm your flight, there should be someone with extensive knowledge in this area. If you are booking through a travel agent, have them check out the facilities available from the airline. If you see some aspect during your journey that needs attention or want to offer a suggestion on how to improve disability facilities, turn to the back of your in-flight magazine. There is usually an address and phone number available for contacting that specific airline. Sometimes there is a dedicated disability assistance hotline.

The Society for Accessible Travel and Hospitality (SATH) is a nonprofit group that provides information on assisting travelers with disabilities. For more information, write:

SATH
347 Fifth Ave., Suite 610
New York, NY 10016
Phone: 212-447-7284
Website: _www.sath.org_

I was proud of that young man. He didn't let his disability interfere with living life to the fullest. He made me want to be more adventurous in life, and I always think of him when I get nervous about doing something new.

In my heart, I am sure he had the time of his life in Europe.

3

Amenities Up in the Air

Bon Appetite

"BEEF OR CHICKEN?" THOSE are the standard choices in an Economy dinner service. Only, when it gets to your row the flight attendant says, "Would you care for beef?"

"No, I'll take the chicken selection," you quickly reply.

"I'm sorry, sir, there are no more chicken entrees, but I have the beef."

You have two options at this point, take the beef and eat what you can (it could surprise you and be quite tasty), or you can get very upset and make a scene.

"It says in my menu that I have the selection of Roast Chicken or Pepper Steak. I would like the Roast Chicken!"

"Yes, sir, but it also says at the bottom that we're sorry if your selection is not available. Believe me when I tell you that I am sorry, but your selection is not available."

The usual reply is "So I don't have a choice?"

"Yes, sir, you do, Yes or No." (It's my favorite comeback.)

Let's discuss for a moment why we run out. Longer flights are stocked with a meal for each passenger and crew with about a 10% over for last-minute passengers and mistakes on special meals. There is no way any airline is going to stock 100% of one choice and 100% of the other. In an attempt to keep wastage to a minimum, the food services cater flights at about 65-45 in favor of the more popular choice. I guarantee that if it's catered at 65 beef, the most popular selection will be chicken, and vice versa, without fail.

Unfortunately, we quite often run out of a selection toward the last rows, and, believe it or not, we actually do feel badly about not giving you your choice. We really appreciate all of you who smile and say it's O.K., even if you don't mean it. For those of you who insist on carrying on and sulking, or causing a fuss, you are just going to have to deal with it. Let's face it, this is a ten-hour flight. In a lifetime of thousands of hours, it is not going to kill you not to have your choice this once. Ironically, the less popular choice is usually the tastier entree.

Special Meals

Ah, something near and dear to every flight attendant's heart. Here's a scenario: A full 747 flight from New York to Paris. Out of approximately 300 people in Economy, 147 have ordered special meals. Out of those 147, 30 percent did not order them but their wives did, or their travel agents made a mistake. Since we are catered almost exactly, some people aren't going to get their special requests, while some are but would rather have the normal meal. Regardless, this special-meal fiasco will add an additional hour to the overall meal service.

Understand one thing, "special meal" doesn't mean special person or special attention. Going on vacation or to a business meeting is not the best time to plan a diet. When you reserve your ticket you may decide to order a low-fat meal and make a good start on the trip. You get on the plane three weeks later; you're handed a menu and think that the Chicken Kiev sounds great. Right? You forgot one thing – your low-fat special meal. So instead of Chicken Kiev, you get a bland piece of warm dried out chicken breast with some rice cakes and a carton of skimmed milk. Yummy!

Some passenger will insist that he didn't order it. Well, yes, he did, and I can prove it with the passenger-seating plan. You probably won't be able to back out of your special meal and get the normal selection, because we are catered almost exactly. Either that or the flight attendant is just miffed that you wasted his or her time with the request. For example: "Mr. Jones, here is your strict vegetarian meal."

"Uhm... Can I have the Sirloin Steak instead?" I doubt that you will get much sympathy there. The whole concept of special meals has gotten out of control.

The following is just a small list of special meals that the passenger has to choose from:

- Kosher (chicken, fish, or beef)
- Low fat, low cholesterol, or low sodium (usually low taste)
- Specialty platters (chef salad, deli platter, cold seafood, fruit plate) also known as yuppy platters
- Children's meals (usually junk food that makes your child hyperactive all flight)
- Special restriction meals (diabetic, lactose intolerant, allergic to spices or nuts, etc.)

The biggest section of them all is the vegetarian: Hindi veg, Western veg, Kosher veg, Kosher low-sodium veg, Kosher low-sodium lactose-free veg, vegetable veg (?), strict veg (vegan), Moslem veg, children's veg; and, get this, there is even the vegetarian deli platter, which, all in all, should be nothing but a pickle.

Don't get me wrong – I do believe that there is a sincere need for special meals, although I don't think the general passenger understands its intent. If you don't really require one, don't order one. Honestly they are generally not as good as the ordinary selection.

If you do require one, make sure you reserve it 48 hours in advance. If you have a special medical condition, or cannot possibly eat an ordinary meal, then bring your own back-up. Don't depend solely on the airline, because you have a 30% chance of not getting it. Big airlines deal with millions of people a day, and if you think your airline of choice is perfect or close to it, then have a nice flight; we will wake you when it's over.

Doing Your Business

THE TOILET, BATHROOM, RESTROOM, loo, bog, john, crapper, the facilities, whatever you want to call it, it's all the same. On the airplane, the proper name for it is the lavatory (or lav, for short). You know, the apparatus that sounds like it's sucking the waste along with your eardrums out into the atmosphere. The sound you hear is not the jettison of sewage; it is the air pressure sucking the waste into the airplane's septic tanks. Just imagine if it was sucked out into the atmosphere, I would have a present for the White House every time I flew over Washington, DC.

It's the one item that everyone on the plane has in common. Oh sure, there are different lavs for the different classes of services, but the Economy passengers sneak up to the ones in Business Class, and the Business Class passengers sneak up to the ones in First Class. For what? A flower and a folded napkin? Is it worth the risk of embarrassment of being told to return to your own class of service? It's just easier when passengers use the facilities in their designated cabin. They aren't any bigger in any specific cabin. The toilet paper is of the same quality. What might be different is that the lavs in the front may be a bit cleaner, because they are used less. It all evens out eventually.

I'd say the biggest problem with the lavs is the lines of people waiting to use them. There is what we call "rush hour traffic" for the toilets. Those times are: after take-off, after the meal, after the movies, and right before landing. Those would be the times to avoid if humanly possible. It doesn't help that some passengers feel that the restrooms are a perfect place to rest, or a great place for a makeover, or a wonderful area to catch up on the news.

Here are a few pieces of lavatory advice:

1. Wear something on your feet at all times. (Men with bad aims are too common.)

2. Check the seal between the door and the lock. (I caught a little boy intensely staring into the door. When I investigated I found he was staring at a young woman changing out of her bodysuit. I locked it off for the remainder of the flight and reported it, but be careful – this happens more than you think.)

3. Do your thing and get out; people will be very thankful.

4. Avoid rush hour; it's not fun to wait too long for necessary functions.

I read the other day that one of the Asian airlines is planning to upgrade its First Class lavatories. This will include windows, soft lighting, and classical music. Why would anyone want to ever come out? The lines will be astronomical, but I can just hear the publicity now:

"Come fly with us, it will be a truly moving experience."

Or how about:

"Fly our airline, the only airline to provide the new service, 'Poo with a View'."

Whether we like it or not, with long flights come dirty toilets. With bad aims, confusing amounts of different papers, and toiletry hygiene, lavatories are bound to get a bit messy.

Flight attendants will attend to general tidying from time to time, and a couple of Asian carriers even have one F/A whose sole purpose is for lavatory cleaning duty at all times. Sounds good, right? Let's talk honestly, folks, do you want someone serving you lunch who just got off lav duty? Think about it.

Some female flight attendants pride themselves on the fact that they don't actually sit down on the toilet seat. They have perfected the art of squatting. (So don't always blame the men for the bad aims.) Pilots on some planes even demand a private lav. It's getting way out of hand. All you need to do is wipe the seat clear with a paper towel and then use a seat liner. Let's not go overboard.

Attention All Mile High Club Members or Applicants

This is always an interesting subject. The famous Mile High Club. Does it exist? Is it common? Some say a daring place to commence intimacy. Well, if you have seen the condition and the size of most restrooms on a long flight, that is the last thing that comes to mind. Although passion is a strong persuader, and, yes, I have caught it happening several times, no, it doesn't happen all the time. It's practically impossible to be undetected, leaving or entering (no pun intended) the bathroom. Usually liquor has played a major role, and nearly everyone knows that alcohol and passion are a dangerous cocktail.

Once there was a young woman afraid of flying, who decided to relieve her fear by drinking. Not accustomed to alcohol, she was caught in the lav twice with two different men (a sleeping pill would have been more effective).

We try to discourage it, but there are always a few...

Myth: The orgasm is ten times more intense because of the cabin pressure and the height of the plane. False, it's just the excitement of possibly getting caught and doing it in a bizarre place... or so I'm told.

Myth: Flight attendants secretly want to join the club with a passenger. False, they could lose their jobs, plus gossip and rumors are so prevalent in their world that it would ruin their lives.

However, an incident I experienced contradicts this. I was in the front of the airplane talking with a few F/As. A man from First Class came out of a nearby toilet. When the door closed, the occupied sign quickly reappeared. Somebody else was obviously in there. All three of us looked at one another in shock and amusement. We decided to wait it out and discover who his accomplice was. We had deduced that it was a certain woman from Business Class. Half an hour went by when the vacant sign came on, the door opened, and out walked a male flight attendant. He smiled and acted like nothing happened, but he knew that we knew, when our jaws hit the floor.

"What?" He smiled. "I don't want this going beyond us, OK, gang?"

We kind of stumbled away, still in shock. He didn't go to the layover hotel with us, but instead went away with his mystery man. I saw them greeted by a black limousine, a wife and two young daughters.

He came back the next day with bite marks on his neck. He blushed as I told him that I just didn't want to know or even think about it. Different strokes for different folks (sorry about that one).

No, the restroom isn't the only place it's done. The blankets on a night flight, hands not in sight, or heads bobbing. Lower kitchen galley, bunkroom, and I even heard of it in the cockpit. Most of the stuff you hear about is exaggeration, but somewhere, somehow, it probably happened.

My 80-year-old grandmother once asked me about the Mile High Club. She had heard the term and didn't know if it was some sort of frequent flier club, good toward mileage points. I explained as delicately as possible.

"Sex in the bathroom?" she exclaimed. "Why, that's impossible, I've been in one, and there isn't enough room to brush your hair much less lie down."

Who says innocence diminishes with age? I left it at that.

Answering the Call

IT'S A SOUND THAT every flight attendant cringes at, dreams of, fears, dreads, tries to ignore, but, nevertheless, answers. It can be the tip of the iceberg, the final straw, and the difference between sanity and insanity. Of course, I am talking about the wonderful invention, the call bell. It's located usually in the worst place possible, next to the volume control for the movie. Which sets off the mistake factor and the curious-kid phenomenon.

When this button is pushed (the one with the male or female figure holding a tray), not only does it illuminate a small light above your seat, but it delivers an unmistakable "PING" sound in the galley (kitchen). One that is just loud enough to get our attention and, if repeated too many times, will drive us bananas.

Now, what you are probably thinking is, "Why not just go out and see what they want?" It sounds simple enough. Well, with 300 people in the Economy section, here is the breakdown of these calls:

70% – Mistakes: Oops, didn't mean to. That's not my reading light?

15% – Curiosity: What does that button do? Kids with itchy fingers.

10% – Thirsty: Can I have a drink? (Which sets off a chain reaction.) My headphones don't work.

4% – Questions: Where are we? What time are we arriving? Can I have cards?

0.9% – Miscellaneous

0.1% – I need help. **That 0.1% is the real reason that button is there.**

There are people who get on a flight and ring their call button three or four times an hour, and others who don't touch it the whole flight.

What people who are constantly ringing don't understand is that we are probably in the process of setting up for a service. When the bell rings we have to drop what we are doing and answer the call light. In the long run it is you who suffers.

Of course, the situation varies in each class of service. Which may sound unfair but, considering the ratio of flight attendants per passenger, it makes sense.

First Class - There is one F/A assigned to every three passengers. You or your business has paid too much for your ticket. Please ring that call button for 100% of your needs. It will give those senior flight attendants something to do with their time.

Business Class - There is one flight attendant assigned to approximately every 12 passengers. The ratio is not so overwhelming, but it can get hectic from time to time. Ring your call button for most things, but if it becomes a regular occurrence, meet us halfway. Come to the galley once in a while. Your legs probably need a good stretch.

Economy Class - There is one flight attendant assigned to every 50 passengers. If it's a crowded flight, please remember that we're working hard to make this an enjoyable flight and to keep you comfortable. If it's not during the service, we probably have a bar set up in the galley. Feel free to come back at any time, and we'll be happy to fix you a drink. The call bell is there mainly for "I have a problem," or especially for "My chest hurts." Or the man next to you is asleep, and you want a drink. Go ahead and ring it once in a while, but just not for everything. What is needed is a little common sense and understanding. Don't get angry if we don't come right away. Our immediate thought is that it's probably a mistake.

I do want to make it very clear that everyone should ring the bell if it is pertaining to any medical problems or safety matters.

The following is an example of a chain reaction scenario:

"PING." I walk up two cabins to answer the call. "Yes, sir, can I help you?"

"Can I have a coke, please?" The man yells from under his headphones.

"Sure." I walk back two cabins, get a coke, and return. "Here you go."

"Thanks a lot, can I have a Bacardi Rum to go with that?"

"All right," I reply, growing a little impatient. Back and forth I go.

"I'm sorry, my wife wants one now." Back and forth again.

"Can I have one, too?" the man in the next aisle exclaims.

Back and forth to find the girl next to him wants an orange juice.

COME ON, FOLKS! Come back to the galley. I know it's my job, but cut me some slack.

I have been on two flights where the call bell was broken, and for ten hours straight we heard the unnerving "PING," "PING," one after another, for the entire flight. A crew member from each flight resigned. I have to admit, I didn't recover for some time afterwards. The airlines are fairly clever not to put a call light reset button within the nearby reach of a flight attendant, because otherwise we wouldn't have to physically go to the seat to turn it off. We'd just reset and hope it was a mistake.

You have a call button in the lavatory. If you push it, we have the right to enter the cubicle (even though it is locked, we have a secret way in) and ensure that you are all right. So, if you don't want anyone interrupting anything personal, then don't push the orange button next to the toilet paper. Just a warning! One time that light was going on and off in a repeating rhythm. We all looked at each other and wondered if it could be...naah. We all investigated anyway.

Moans were coming from the toilet on the left side. "Are you OK?" we asked in a low voice, but no response came from the lavatory. The bell kept on ringing but at a faster pace.

We opened the door and found two new members of the Mile High Club, stark naked and not realizing that they were bumping against the call button. The lady spotted us first and began to scream.

The man whispered, "Sshhhh, somebody will hear us."

They blushed for the remaining six hours, but were good sports, so we gave them a bottle of champagne and two membership cards to the Mile High Club.

A Sunset for the Books

THERE ARE THOSE PASSENGERS who insist on a window seat because of the head support that the wall of the plane provides. They close the window shade and never look out that porthole the entire flight. They are oblivious to many wondrous sights, such as the Northern Lights, icebergs off Greenland, Caribbean islands, the land patterns, the cloud formations, the moon, the sun, the world, to name only a few.

This is a story of my greatest venture out of that window. It was a chilly November afternoon in London, and I was ready to get back home to California. I was working in Economy, and, to our amazement, we were only half full. A break from the usual oversold, crammed in, "body in every seat" flight. It was highly unusual for any of the West Coast bound flights to leave with one empty seat, much less 50%, but who was I to look a gift horse in the mouth?

It couldn't have come at a better time, because I was somewhat depressed about my life just then, and didn't care for a stressful flight. It was about 3:30 p.m. when we took off as the sun started to set. In London, the winter days are short, so that was a typical time. It was a beautiful sunset. The clouds in the distance looked like glowing pieces of charcoal. The timing was quite convenient because, usually whenever I got depressed, I would go to the beach and visit the sunset. This time the sunset came to me. I was afraid that I was going to miss the best part during the service, but it never quite went away, because we were flying into it.

Two hours later I took a seat by the window and watched the loveliest skyline that I could remember. How long would this scenic display last? I went into the cockpit to get a better view, and the whole sky was a glowing masterpiece. The captain said that we might just get lucky and have the sunset the whole way there.

My fellow F/As were justifiably annoyed with my lack of help, but we weren't full, and there was no way I was going to miss this. My mind wandered through the skyline working out any depression and filling me with inner joy.

Pink moment after pink moment, it felt like a religious experience. The pilots felt it, too. Nobody talked or made a sound for the longest time. The beauty in the skyline mesmerized us all. The only time depression returned was when I had to go back to work. I didn't want to leave and miss the final farewell of the sun, but duty called. After the second service, I raced back up to the cockpit to get the last trace of beauty, if there was any left.

To my surprise, the sky was erupting once again. As we approached Los Angeles the sun put on its grand finale. The beauty climaxed and sent fireworks over the entire skyline. Los Angeles looked like a true city of angels. Of course, I knew that it was the smog and pollution that created all the various colors, but chose not to think of that point just then. I was close to tears of awe when the display sank into the sea.

I deplaned rejuvenated, full of vigor and glad to be alive. Unfortunately three hours of bumper-to-bumper traffic erased any of that sentiment.

4

Unexpected Encounters

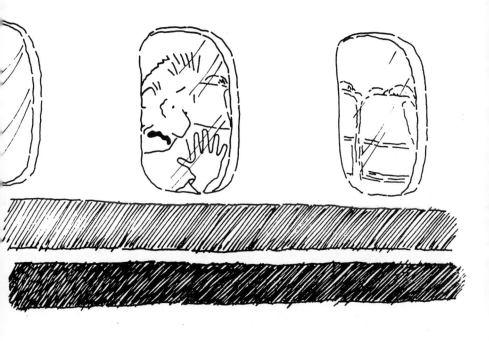

It's All Greek to Me

I FIND THAT IN foreign places, the best experiences take place spontaneously, and the unexpected happens. It's not something that is planned, timed, or counted on. I can fondly recall my adventure on a Greek island as an example. It was not quite the tourist season, but the sun was unaware of that fact and beamed down regardless.

Unfortunately, it seemed that every tourist and local on the island was romancing someone. Everyone, that is, but me. I had broken up with my girlfriend the night before leaving, but I decided to go on the vacation anyway.

At first, I was a bit skeptical of going to Greece for the first time, alone, but I felt very liberated. I knew my ex-girlfriend expected me not to go. This way she could wonder who I had gone with. So I took the island by storm on a rented moped and brought along a good book, just in case I needed something to occupy my time. I caught several couples at different beaches skinny-dipping and making love in the sunset. Everywhere I turned, loneliness seemed to slap me in the face.

One day I decided to take a tourist charter trip to a nearby island. It was known for its stunning ivory beaches and a hotel palace. There were boat trips every other hour, and I figured it would be good to get off the main island for a while. It took about two hours by boat to get there. The scenery was breathtakingly beautiful, and the mixture of ocean air and the sun's vibrancy refreshed my soul.

When we arrived at the small island I soon realized that they weren't kidding in their description. It was one big white ivory beach. It consisted of a fishing port, a hotel in the shape and size of a castle, and a duty-free shop, which was closing, due to a half-day schedule. The manager of the hotel where I was staying asked me to pick him up a 2-liter bottle of ouzo (Greek liquor) at the duty-free shop. I made my purchase and headed for a secluded spot to relax and grab some sun. They were giving tours of the hotel, but I had seen enough hotels in my job.

Just about everyone was sunbathing in the nude, and, although I had never tried it before, I thought that I would give it a shot. Despite my new lack of inhibition, I looked for a secluded spot. I listened to my personal stereo and settled into my book. Some people walked by, and some became my neighbors. But strangely enough I didn't feel inhibited or shy. I dozed off with a smile on my face.

I awoke a couple of hours later to a gentle yet persistent tap on my shoulder. Through the now fading sunlight, I could see a glossy cap of golden brown curls, framing a tender bronzed face with jade green eyes. She was sweetly smiling, gazing at my now brick-red body unabashedly.

"I'm sorry to disturb you, sir, but are you staying here at the hotel?" she asked in broken English.

Not quite awake, I replied, "Uh, no. I'm just here for the day. Why?"

"Well the last boat off the island is about to leave. You will have to hurry to catch it.

I stood up and saw the boat in the distance, about 400 yards away, preparing to depart. I also discovered that I was standing naked in front of this pretty young woman – not only naked, but with my sails at half mast. I got dressed in a hurry, trying not to appear embarrassed, and willing my sails to recede. She even handed me pieces of my clothing; it was a team effort. I ran for the boat at full steam, but the boat pulled away, halfway through my sprint.

The young woman caught up to me, although I prayed that she would not. She introduced herself as Dimitria, and handed me a sock I had dropped mid dash. She told me to come with her because she had an idea. There were no vacancies in the hotel, plus, at $200 a night, I would have to sleep on the beach. We walked around the hotel to a tiny little fishing pier, where a dilapidated boat was moored, and three older Greek fishermen were unloading their catch. She knew one of them and began talking in Greek.

All of a sudden, a silence hit them. They all turned my way and scowled. The eldest one shook his head and lit his freshly rolled cigarette. They argued a bit between them, then nodded. I didn't think they wanted me on their boat, but that was okay with me. I wasn't sure how seaworthy that boat was. Have you ever heard the stories of those tourists that were never heard from again? This was a perfect scenario.

Dimitria returned and said, "They are going back to the main island in 30 minutes and have agreed to take you along for the equivalent of ten US dollars. Under the conditions that you don't get seasick easily, and realize that they only have enough food for themselves."

"Great," I replied hesitantly.

"Don't worry, the eldest one is my grandfather."

During those 30 minutes she stayed and talked with me. She told me that she worked at the hotel, but lived not far from where I was staying on the main island. She returned home on the weekends. We arranged an informal date in two days time, if I made it there in one piece. Since she had already seen me naked, I didn't feel that a date was out of the question. The grandfather began to give me dirty looks as we said good-bye.

We pushed off with about three hours of sun left. The radio belted out Greek music from three rickety speakers. They must have been a bit deaf, considering the volume. It was a four-hour journey, and supposedly none of them spoke a word of English. I spoke even less Greek. So I kept quiet, enjoying the dance of the many hues in a most memorable sunset. The sun hung over the edge of the ocean like a giant orange slipping into the water.

Two hours into the journey, I got a bit bored and thought I might break the ice. I opened my backpack and pulled out the bottle of ouzo that was supposed to be for my hotel manager. I held it up in a gesture of friendship. One looked at me in shock as he yelled to the other two. One ran off the deck and down to the galley below. Maybe I had offended them. Maybe they didn't drink.

The man reappeared with drinking glasses and a wide toothless grin on his face. The other two laughed, and we opened the bottle and began to drink. Although they knew that we didn't speak each other's language, it didn't stop them from chatting away to me as if I understood. So I answered them back in English, on what I had imagined them asking me. One thing was for certain: all of us were getting quite drunk. They sang to the Greek songs on the radio, and I tried their foul, harsh cigarettes as the sun set peacefully in the distance. Then a miracle happened. A song came on the radio that I knew and loved. A Bob Marley song, "No Woman, No Cry."

They seemed to get excited as if they knew it. Although they spoke zero English, they knew the words by heart, as I did. So there we were, drunk as skunks, arm-in-arm, sailing between the Greek islands, and singing – no, yelling out – a great song.

The eldest one had the final line and it went like this: "No wooomain noh (glug glug glug) craaihhh!!" And with a semi-toothless smile, he polished off our bottle.

We got to shore laughing and chattering away like the best of friends. I fell off the boat and onto the pier with a roar of laughter. I bid them farewell and staggered toward my bed.

Two days of a hangover and an embarrassing sunburn later, I met up with Dimitria. We hit it off immediately. I already had her grandfather's thumbs-up as he instructed her to bring me along to one of their family parties. What looked like a disastrous trip at first turned out to be one of my fondest memories.

One-Way Ticket

THE LADY SEATED NEXT to me coughed and hacked away during the entire boarding of the flight to Miami. I was on my way to see friends and soak in the sun, and I was sure this lady was going to give me the worst cold of my life.

About 50 years old with short blonde hair, she was pretty enough, but years of smoking had drained her face and left her with a raspy voice. She smelt of cigarettes, and I realized then it wasn't a cold I was going to catch, but maybe a phlegm bath. Her agonizing cough made me uncomfortable, so I politely looked around for an empty seat to move to, but the entire flight was full.

At first she wasn't very talkative, but after her nicotine withdrawal started to kick in, she was all mouth.

"Why are all domestic flights non-smoking?" she asked in frustration.

"Probably the lawsuits," I replied.

"You may be right."

"Sounds like you need to take it easy on the cigarettes anyway," I said, amazed that I could be so bold, and feared her justified retaliation.

She just chuckled and said, "It's a bit too late for me now. I'm on a one-way ticket. You see, I'm on my way to Miami to die." She continued, "My doctor gave me about one, maybe two months. No family left, a dog that won't miss me. The hell if I'm going to spend it in bad weather." She attempted a half smile as she took a full gulp of her bourbon on the rocks.

"I'm sorry, I didn't mean to offend you," I kindly sympathized, but felt like curling up into a ball and disappearing.

"No, it's okay, you didn't know. Plus, I have more or less come to grips with it. Probably a good thing considering my time frame."

"Well, maybe if you didn't smoke while you're there you might have more time than you think," I said, not even attempting to comprehend what she was going through.

"That's the funny thing, I'm not dying of lung cancer, but of an inoperable brain tumor. Anyway, why would you want to live longer with the knowledge that you're dying?" She stared out of the window, and went into a trance.

"Doesn't everyone live with that knowledge every day?" I stated, trying to be deep.

"Good point," she mused, and ordered another bourbon.

I joined her.

We talked, laughed, and cried together the entire flight. It was truly an enlightening experience. I felt a special bond between us, and was sad that she was not long for this world. I questioned my own mortality and only hoped that if it were my time, I would be able to spend my final days in the same fashion.

The plane landed and the flight was over, but I did not want to say good-bye. I had just met this person, but in that short time she had become a part of me. Perhaps, it was because I wasn't dying, or perhaps it was the bourbon that was dramatizing the event. Whatever it was, I felt a special love for her.

We walked off the plane together and through the airport, chatting away about our plans and concluded our discussion.

"I would give you my address to write, but I doubt I will get it, plus I doubt you could afford the postage." She hugged me and whispered into my ear, "Enjoy it while you're here." She wiped the tear off her cheek, turned and walked away, disappearing into the crowds of people swarming the airport.

I try to remember this story when I am faced with day-to-day troubles and the heartaches of life. I hope she had a pleasant, or should I say peaceful, time in Miami, and wherever she is now, I thank her, and won't ever forget her.

Welcome Aboard

WE ARRIVED AT THE gate about five p.m. for our 11-hour flight back to the U.S. only to discover that we had a half-hour delay due to a mechanical problem. We immediately became suspicious, because "half hour" and "delay" don't belong in the same sentence. We were asked to go on board, and do our preflight checks. We would be told later when passenger boarding would commence. Exactly half an hour later the passengers were boarded, so we assumed the problem was fixed. Wrong!

Every half hour, an announcement was made stating that it would be yet another half hour. This went on for three hours, until our legalities grew short. F/As have a contract that specifies how many hours we are allowed, by law, to work on board an aircraft. This prevents aircrews from being flown until they are so tired they could not possibly evacuate an aircraft safely. Two minutes before we became illegal the ground staff closed the doors, and the plane pushed back. Yes, we were tired, but we were happy to be on our way.

Wrong again! They had removed the jetway – the movable tunnel that connects the airplane to the airport, to prevent the crew from walking off, and continued to work on the plane. An hour later the problem still wasn't fixed. The only thing the mechanics were able to do was break the plane's air conditioning system. Three hundred people started to sweat all at once as tempers flared.

While we were waiting, a passenger suddenly had an epileptic seizure. The passenger needed further medical attention and needed to be off-loaded, so we had to be pushed back to the gate, which took 45 minutes.

They took the passenger off, but meanwhile the crew had long since become illegal and demanded to get off the plane. The gate agent replied that it was impossible – there was no replacement crew, no vacant hotels in the city, and they had fixed the problem.

"Oh no, they haven't," a voice shouted from out of the cockpit.

"Out of the way, we know our contractual rights," two senior F/As yelled, as they stormed off the plane.

Furiously, the gate agent got on to the microphone and made the following announcement:

"Ladies and gentlemen: Thanks to your flight attendants, this flight has to be canceled until tomorrow. At this time, we are unsure of any vacant hotels due to the conventions taking place, so bring your pillows and blankets off the plane with you and prepare for the worst." (She has since been fired.)

As the passengers got off, they hurled endless verbal abuse, threatened, shoved; one elderly passenger even spat in a crew member's face.

The airport security manager greeted us. He informed us of the mini-riot that was occurring in the departure lounge. We would have to be smuggled out of the airport the back way with a police escort.

We got to a hotel with plenty of rooms at 1:30 in the morning. I went to the soda machine and got several dirty sneers from some of the passengers who were put up at the same hotel. Departure was supposed to be at 12:30 the next day, but the plane was still not fixed, so the flight was delayed again until 5 p.m.

The passengers got on around 5:30, not at all happy, but just wanting to get on. The plane pushed back and rolled along the runway. We said our belated farewells to the airport. Or so we thought. When we got to the end of the runway, the captain made an announcement informing us that we would be returning to the gate because of a warning indicator light on the left engine. Three hundred passengers growled in their seats; some cried, some yelled.

Two hours later, we finally took off, praying for an uneventful flight, which we knew wouldn't happen.

Halfway through the meal service, we discovered that 60 percent of the entree dishes were empty, and we could only hand out the trays, which consisted of a salad, a roll, and a melted dessert. We gave away all the crew meals, but were still short. Two hours after that the audio broke, so nobody could hear the movie or the music. We then discovered that all of the economy toilets would not flush, so everyone had to use the four lavatories in the front. A line formed on each side of the plane, starting at First Class and stretching to the middle of Economy. At one point, I couldn't take it any longer, so I hid in one of the broken toilets, just to get away from the abuse.

The stench of the backed up sewage was nothing compared to the insults that were being thrown at us. I was a grown man hiding in a toilet from an angry mob.

What did I do to deserve this? How did I get to this place in time? A flight attendant? What was I thinking? I was wearing a name tag and a tie that matched the curtains on the airplane. Everyone has a time when they question their existence in life. This was mine.

I thought back to the time when I started this whole airline ordeal. I went to the job interview out of curiosity. I spoke another language, was unsure of my major at university, loved to travel and thought it would be an adventure. I thought it might be a small break from college. Thousands of people were lining up for interviews. I didn't fancy my chances, but before I knew it I was on an airplane to Miami, headed for training. Was I crazy dropping out of a big-name university for a $1,000 a month waiter-in-the-sky job? Had I just made the biggest mistake of my life?

We arrived at the training center, and I spied seven or eight South American girls with study books in hand, and the skimpiest of bikinis, walking in from the pool. They had been studying by the pool for the better part of the day.

I raised my head and looked toward the heavens and said, "Thank You, Lord, I think I'm gonna like it here."

I was soon to discover that 50% of the trainees wouldn't make it to graduation, fraternization was not allowed, and all three of my new roommates were gay. It wasn't as easy as I expected. But after perfecting the art of faking a smile 24 hours a day, and a little fashion sense from my roommates, I graduated Charm School and headed off to my base. I was truly in for a different kind of adventure. It was going to be an adventure that I could do for a couple of years before I went back to reality. Or so I thought.

The broken toilet in which I was performing my reality check had started to back up and become intolerable. I put on my bulletproof face, emerged from the smelly cubicle, and tried not to let the rude comments sink in. One of my colleagues actually quit in the middle of the flight and remained in the cockpit for the duration. (She had a nervous breakdown.)

Each hour seemed like an eternity. The flight appeared endless, and the passenger abuse never eased. We got closer to our destination, but joined a holding pattern for two hours until the captain declared an Emergency Priority Landing. The airplane limped into the gate. We were desperate to put this catastrophe behind us, but lo and behold, the jetway broke. It took another 45 minutes until they pulled up the temporary stairs and let off the angry mob. All of the flight attendants hid in the bathrooms, rather than smile and say good-bye. I wasn't fast enough as all of the toilets were taken, so I was forced to take more abuse. Everyone was furious. I mentally flinched at every comment.

"I'm never flying this crappy airline again," many said as they stormed off the plane.

"After this flight, I wouldn't either," was the only response I could offer.

A little old lady was the last to get off. She smiled, gave me a quarter, and said, "You tried your hardest, and I know it wasn't easy. Thank you, sonny."

I nearly burst into tears at that very moment. I got home, opened a bottle of red wine, and laid in a hot bath for three hours.

If you're ever on a flight that goes wrong, remember this one, and consider yourself lucky. Just when you think that it can't get much worse, watch out, because it just might.

Dancing in Berlin

MY FAVORITE LAYOVER HAS to be a trip I had in November of 1989. I was flying into Berlin, and the captain made the following announcement:

"Ladies and gentlemen, we are extremely pleased to inform you that the German government has just signed a Declaration of Unification. The Berlin Wall is now obsolete."

I thought that the captain was making a joke or had lost his marbles. I went to the cockpit to see what was up and to hear it for myself. It was true. Unfortunately, we remained in a holding pattern for a while, because the air traffic controllers had started the celebration early.

Could this be possible? There was no rumor in the media of this occurring. I just couldn't believe it. The crew and I decided to send our bags on to the hotel and head down to the Brandenburg Gate to check it out for ourselves. Sure enough, when we got there, there were thousands of people celebrating, cheering, and crying for joy.

It was one huge party. People I didn't know came up to me and hugged me, I wasn't German, but I don't think it really mattered. People were dancing on the Wall, while we joined the masses that were hacking away for souvenirs. Unfortunately, all we had were our house keys, but they sufficed.

It was cold out, so we gathered around the singing crowds and drank gluwein (hot mulled wine) and pretended to know the words. CBS was there to film the spectacular event, and filmed our group singing away. Afterwards, we realized that we were filmed drinking in uniform (a big no-no, but oh well).

We were a part of history being made. It was a day that will be remembered for hundreds and hundreds of years to come. Many people died trying to get over, under, and through that Wall. The daughter of one of those victims was in floods of tears in the group that I was singing and drinking with.

After four hours we got tired and took a taxi to the hotel. We thawed out on the way, as did our hands, which had begun to bleed from the preserved scraps of souvenir picking. We all laughed and tried not to bleed over our pieces of the Wall and the poor man's taxi cab. We were a ghastly sight when we checked into the hotel, and were a bit worried that they would give us a hard time, but I don't think that anyone in Germany was sober on that night.

I sent 20 pieces of the Wall to different friends and family that year for Christmas. Unfortunately, half of them thought I was joking and threw them away.

Germany is united now, and evidence of it ever being separate is gone. The people from the east side came over to see what all the commotion was about, and promptly returned home. The Wall is gone now, but the memories and the evil that it represented will live on forever. The remains have been boxed up and sold off at department stores all over the world. Hey, they always said freedom had its price.

It will stand out as my favorite layover of all times, for I was indeed a part of history in the making.

Reserved

ONE OF THE BIGGEST DRAWBACKS to this job has to be the aspect of "reserve." If you are junior enough, you will have to endure the agony and instability of not knowing where you are going and when. It is called reserve because in the event that someone calls in sick, or an irregular operation occurs, they have F/As ready for use. The F/As on reserve have been categorized as "just-in-case."

We hate reserve because we can't plan a month, week, or even a day in advance. You have certain days you are on and off. But when you are on, you could be called up at any time and be used on any trip. Many F/As have other jobs or go to school, but on reserve that is practically impossible. Flight schedulers never sleep, so they are known to call you at all hours of the night. You end up showering with a beeper and sleeping with one eye open. Of course, with the advent of cellular phones, reserve has grown more comfortable to bear.

Many airlines have different methods of reserve, but generally you will find the senior F/As exempt. Which is only fair, considering they have probably paid their dues previously. It is funny when I see flight attendants who have been flying for over 25 years sitting reserve. It means that they are from a popular base and, compared to their flying partners, are more junior. At one base, reserve may start at two years and under, but at others, 30 years and under can be the norm.

When I flew for Pan Am, I actually liked reserve. I was new and thought it exciting not to know where in the world I would be going that day. Sure, I had to sit by the phone and be cooped up in my apartment all day (mobile phones were for the rich back then), but when that phone rang, my heart would always jump. It was like Christmas.

"Ah, hello, this is the crew desk and you have been assigned flight 184 departing at 17:30, returning in seven days time, at 06:30."

"Where am I going?" I would blurt out in anticipation.

"Moscow."

It would fill me with joy, especially if I had never been there before. I would get calls for Budapest, Zurich, Germany, Paris, Italy, and Rio de Janeiro, to name only a few.

The service was hard, but I was getting paid for going on an all-expenses paid trip somewhere exotic. Unfortunately, flying with other airlines has become more routine, layovers not as long or exotic. I now have a life outside of flying, so I am lucky not to have to be on reserve.

Reserve these days can be frightening. You could be called at two in the morning for a 6 o'clock flight and work from Atlanta to Frankfurt and think you're finished. But then you find out that they want you to work a flight that same day from Frankfurt to Athens. If you are legal, then you have no say in the matter.

Greece, great, huh? Not really, considering that you have a 13-hour layover, only to work back to Frankfurt to join your old crew back to Atlanta. Not a fun way to spend three days.

"Hey, how was Greece?"

"The hotel was nice, I think!"

Like death and taxes, for junior F/As in the flying world, reserve is another of life's dreaded sure things.

The Golden Years

IT WAS SCHEDULED TO be a fairly empty flight one chilly November night. I was forced into working the First Class cabin because nobody else wanted to, and I was the most junior. Nobody wanted to work that cabin because we were expecting two VIPs, which usually meant executives or CEOs full of demands and a need for special attention. To my surprise, they turned out to be a sweet elderly couple. They were on their 75th wedding anniversary, and the airline had given them a free First Class ticket around the world.

Her name was Althea. She was 96, dressed in yellow, quite lively for her age, and she was wearing a sunflower in her hair. His name was Earl. He was 94, a bit frail, but he sported a brand new suit and wide ear-to-ear smile.

How amazing, I thought, to spend 75 years with the same person. I was at the point in my life that I didn't think things like that were remotely possible. My relationships were lasting six months at the most. My father was on his sixth marriage, and divorce was starting to become the world's biggest pastime. They truly gave me new hope.

Since it was an empty flight, I watched them from beyond the curtain behind them. This wasn't merely an endurance test for them; they truly loved each other. When they ate, they talked and laughed, unlike so many married couples these days who are void of all conversation. After 75 years they hadn't run out of things to say to each other. I was in awe.

Earl was full of jokes, his favorite being, "I always did like older women." He asked for his second cognac at the end of the meal, which got them quibbling a bit, but it was all in fun. Althea got out her knitting, and he prepared for the movie. The whole crew had joined me in sneaking many peeks at our anniversary couple.

It was a romantic tale of love and life. They had known one other since the age of four and six, for a total of **ninety** years. They'd seen the best and worst of times, the Great Depression, extreme poverty and sickness. They were their first and only loves, the result being **one hundred and fourteen** descendants, and had enjoyed **seventy-five** years of marriage.

Earl leaned over to Althea, and I could just make out the words "I love you," followed by a loving kiss. The crew sighed in unison, and a lump stuck in my throat.

When the flight was over Earl smiled and said "Good-bye, we'll see you on our hundredth anniversary."

I have since been lucky enough to find my Althea and have every intention of modeling our marriage after theirs – although I am not so sure that I will last until age 94. Who knows, the way things are going, I might still be pushing a cart down the aisle hawking "Beef or Chicken."

5

Seating Smart, Stupid

First Class

TO CALL IT ANY other name would be foolish. It's the top of the top, the best of the best, and ultimately, one of the biggest wastes of money, ever. An international round trip ticket starts out at around five thousand dollars, and tops out at around twelve. You're not even buying the seat, just using it for a while.

What do you get for that vast amount of money? You get a huge seat that practically lays out into a bed. The best of champagnes, wines, expensive spirits, gourmet foods, personalized service, and much more. The prominent stars, presidents of companies, business executives, politicians, the filthy rich, and the lucky upgrades sit in this section.

Is it worth it? No, but if you've got money to blow, then do it. There are people in this world with more money than sense, so if you are one of us...I mean them...then I recommend it. Otherwise, sit in Economy and buy yourself a new car when you get to your destination.

Did you know that a cabin full of First Class passengers pays for all expenses, workers' pay, fuel, airplane lease, catering, etc., for that flight? All the rest of the cargo and passengers are profit for the airline.

Did you also know, that usually only one-quarter of a full First Class is paying the fare for their ticket? The others are upgrades, top frequent flyer members, or employees of the airline.

It's hard to compete in this area with the new technology that's coming out. Private cabins, videophones, bathrooms with windows, foot massages, and gambling casinos are just a few innovations that are trying to get your First Class business.

The service has a different cart for each course – setup, appetizer, caviar, tossed salad, entree, fruit and cheese, dessert, liqueurs and fancy chocolates. You get pampered, via one-to-one service.

When I fly First Class, I find it a bit too much. I get tired of saying that I don't want anything else (I don't think they believe me). It's great fun, though, to pretend you're a big wig and to try the exotic offerings. Get tipsy on Dom Perignon, pretend you like Russian caviar, sip a 50-year old Scotch, stuff yourself with unpronounceable foods, fall asleep in a seat more comfortable than your own bed, and wake up with a hangover to freshly squeezed orange juice at your fingertips. It's a wonderful way to fly, but still in my eyes not worth it.

I don't like working in First Class because there is little, if any, personal interaction. A 12-hour flight bores me to tears when I work up there. The passengers want the service and privacy. Idle chitchat, but nothing too personal. Unfortunately, I will take almost all of the hassles they can give me, because if something went wrong, and I was paying that kind of money, I'd be angry as well.

You will normally find the older F/As up there, because it's easier to work, and seniority prevails. The more senior F/As would rather be bored than work any day.

It's not a perfect class of service, and some airlines have got it down better than others. If you look hard enough, you will find its faults. But if you try to find them, you won't enjoy the service, thus wasting your money even more. The bottom line is, it is just a mode of transportation. We are designed to get you from point A to point B, and back again. If you're sitting up there, then you want more than that mode. Hopefully, you'll get it.

If you have always dreamed of flying First Class and finally get your chance, you will probably be disappointed in some way. I guess the same could be said about most dreams.

Upgrade, Anyone?

YOU SEE THEM BESIDE the check-in counter hoping for a response: businessmen, young ladies, frequent flyers, first timers, off-duty employees, and previously inconvenienced passengers. They are the last ones to board, but the first ones to check beyond the curtains to see if there are any available seats. They are the first to cause a fuss if denied, but if rewarded their prize they cause an even bigger fuss, because most of the time they want the world.

They are the upgrades, and they are around for every flight. This phenomenon falls in with the ways of humanity: everyone always strives for something better. Or maybe it is a new trend: get more for free, and to hell with self-respect.

Well, it doesn't always work, and, consequently, it makes some of them very upset. If you are one of these people, you must realize that people won't pay for what they can get for free. If we upgraded everyone, we would never make any money from the Business or First Class fares. Don't get mad that you're not sitting farther forward, especially if you didn't pay for it. Let's be sensible about things.

"My reading light doesn't work, my seat doesn't recline, I smell smoke, I have asthma, diarrhea, epilepsy, heart condition. I am too tall, fat, old. I lost my boarding card, and the ground agent said I could take a seat anywhere. I hate this airline, love this airline. I work for another airline, I am an employee for this airline. My sister's ex-boyfriend's doctor's cousin's daughter used to fly for this airline." These are just some of the many lame attempts to get an upgrade. They never work. Well, almost never. A man had a heart attack, and we had a fairly empty First Class. We moved him up there until we landed, but that's a pretty tough way to get more leg room. My guess is that he was just dying for an upgrade (sorry).

I have had ladies and gentlemen shake my hand upon boarding and hand me twenties, fifties, and even hundred dollar bills asking me to "see what I can do for them." I even had a lady promise to induct me into the Mile High Club if I got her a higher-class seat.

Listen, folks! It's not that we don't want to, it's just plain and simple: *we can't.* Our rules of conduct state specifically that upgrading (without permission from a supervisor on the ground or, in emergencies, from the captain) is an offense punishable by immediate discharge. It's a firm rule, with no room for negotiation or interpretation. Of course, there will always be people who will make their phony excuses and feeble-minded attempts.

You should take something into consideration. You could have an airline employee eating right out of your hand, but when the magic word or implication of an upgrade arises, an alarm bell goes off in their heads which discredits everything you have said up to that point. You've been made. We call it our BS alert.

If you really want an upgrade and are about to attempt to make a scene, remember that a more effective method is to just come right out with it and courteously ask a ground agent. They are more likely to reward simple honesty than wasting their time.

Here are some factors that will increase your chances of getting an upgrade:

1. The flight is oversold in Economy, and there are empty seats in Business and/or First Class.

2. You are a member of that specific airline's frequent flyer mileage club.

3. You are dressed smartly or in business attire. Jacket and tie for men and a dress or suit for women.

4. You are traveling alone. Sorry if you're with kids – it's almost an immediate disqualifier.

5. Always be willing to move when asked. I know of a man who

refused to move because he was seated on the aisle. What he didn't realize was that the seat they were asking him to move to was in First Class.

6. If you have been seriously inconvenienced on a previous flight, make sure the check-in agents know about it. Don't go and make a scene, or they will put you in a seat that is the worst possible one, hoping never to see you again.

7. Courtesy and kindness do go a long way in this industry – I have seen many people upgraded just by the kindness they showed. I know when I am aboard, if someone is especially nice I want to do something extra for him or her, and I'm positive the ground staff feel the same way.

8. Unfortunately, it is also whom you know. If you have a friend at the check-in counter, they will do their best to get you up front. It usually always works.

In conclusion, many people pay a lot of money to sit up front and actually hope for some space and privacy to relax, conduct business, or even sleep. Part of their expectation is not to have a full load all the time, so the airline that upgrades all the time will lose their revenue passengers and the millions associated with them.

Hey, go ahead and try for the upgrade, but I encourage you not to make a scene. The only person you'll embarrass is yourself. Also please remember, I don't make the rules, but I do have to follow them.

Business Class

THIS CLASS IS GENERALLY referred to as Business Class, but the new trend is for the airlines to rename it. For instance, there is: Upper Class, Comfort Class, Diamond Class, Raffles Class, Club World, Myapur, Connoisseur, Club Empress, Magnifico Class, etc. There is even a class that refers to the angle of the seat, called Espace 127.

Why not call them all simply Business Class? There is also a new trend underway which combines Business and First Class, and calling it appropriately Business First – eliminating First Class and making just one fancier form of Business Class.

Business Class got its name because most businesses do not want to pay for First Class, but do not want their employees to have to suffer the hardship of Economy. Most of this section is filled with passengers on business, people who have a bit extra to spend, up and coming stars, employees of the airline, and upgrades. There aren't many crying babies or bare feet wandering in this section.

In comparison with Economy, the seats are bigger and more comfortable, the service is more attentive, and the quality of food is generally better and more substantial. There are premium champagnes, choices of several different reds and whites in your wine selection, CD audio, private video, special amenity kits, newspapers, and more overall space. It's an atmosphere more conducive for sleeping or doing business.

The airline's most frequent flyers and highly regarded customers sit in this cabin. The dreaded "Wanna-Be's" sit here as well. The "Wanna-Be" is referred to as the passenger who got an upgrade from Economy and wants everything we have to offer, and yet more.

Alternatively, there are the passengers who "wanna-be" in First Class, but didn't get the upgrade that they tried so hard for. They typically ask for things only found in First Class, and continue to walk up there quite frequently to use the lavatory, or to see if there was indeed a spare seat for their denied upgrade. "Wanna-Be's" usually criticize the service for its entire duration, trying to prove that they belong in First Class. All that is accomplished is the confirmation of their "pain in the ass" status.

With all the characters and aspects aside, it is a better class of service, but does the price outweigh the services received? The price is generally two and a half times the fare paid in Economy. I would personally rather take a friend along, sit in the back, and have a little extra spending money. Some may have the extra money and enjoy the extra comfort, and consider it worth it. I fly Business Class all the time, but that's because I don't pay for it. If I did, I would be schlepping in the back with the fellow Economians.

For some, it's a status symbol. They might consider themselves superior people; they would never be caught dead sitting with the common people. (Another example of a Wanna-Be.)

With businesses geared more for savings, many businessmen are now finding their tickets in coach. Instead of collecting free trips with mileage club points, they're purchasing upgrades. Businessmen and women usually choose their airline by its frequent flyer clubs and perks. They fly on business and collect points for their personal life. It doesn't matter how badly the airline might treat them; once they have a considerable amount of points, they are usually locked in.

Frequent flyers can give free flights to their family members, or they can just save them for retirement. I know a man who saved so many points that he had five years of free flights ahead of him. So, needless to say, he was a little more than pissed off when the airlines gave frequent flyers a time limit in which to use their points. I think he ended up taking his whole family of ten to Australia, First Class.

If you're not a member of an airline's mileage club, then you are making a big mistake. You're just giving the airline more money. The airline compensates for the free trip awards in the price of a ticket. In a sense, you're paying for it already.

One round trip from Los Angeles to Bombay, India, yields enough points for a free round trip within the United States. Alternately, if you want to try a higher class of service, you could use the points for an upgrade. Just ask your flight attendant for an application. Fill it out, and send it in with a photocopy of your ticket receipt, and you will get credit for that flight.

No, you don't have to fly that airline from then on; you can be a member of several different mileage clubs. The biggest excuse is that you don't travel that much. I have heard that one a thousand times, but you travel more than you may think. Remember when Auntie Flossie died last spring, and you had to fly out to New York? Well, that was 5,000 points right there. I'm sure she would have wanted you to get those points. Don't give more money to the airline; enroll right now! Push that call button....Better yet, get up and get an application in the back.

Switching Seats

IT HAS BECOME A TALENT with frequent flyers, a perfected art for the less inhibited, and a lucky strike for bold first timers. Getting spare seats, or even that whole row next to you, is not a total luck of the draw as most might think. How many times have you come across this scenario: the airplane is completely full, apart from nine seats, but those nine seats have only three people in them and they are stretched out and conveniently slumbering away? Dumb luck? Did they pay for those extra seats? No, they have perfected the technique that we shall call "seat shuffling." I am going to attempt to teach you this method, so perhaps next time it will be you enjoying a whole row to yourself.

Unfortunately, when the flight you are on is completely full, you are almost certainly stuck with the seat that you were assigned. When the flight isn't full, there are definite reasons to switch and certain tricks of the trade to learn.

The Top Ten Reasons to Switch Seats

1. The crying and yelling baby right next to you looks as if it should have been named Damien, and its head is about to start spinning around.

2. The smell of someone around you – rotting feet, gas, or a bad case of body odor – is more than you can handle.

3. Your reading light or movie audio isn't working, and it's a night flight.

4. The lady next to you has her eyes wide open, and every time you move she yells, "What was that?"

5. The man next to you keeps chanting and swatting at imaginary flies.

6. An elderly man sits down next to you, and you get drunk from his breath.

7. The young man sitting next to you is dressed in a cutoff shirt, shorts, and flip-flops. And he boarded the plane singing, "You gotta fight, for your right, to PAARRRTTYY!"

8. A suspicious-looking man is sweating profusely and holding onto his suitcase with all of his might, not releasing it to anyone, nor storing it overhead. (For that matter, it might be a good idea to switch flights.)

9. You board, and notice your seat partner is in handcuffs. The man next to him is wearing sunglasses, and his hand is permanently attached to his inside pocket.

10. You've got a headache, and the person sitting next to you starts to tell you his life story from age three.

Now, going about switching seats has several different approaches. First, you have to find out if the flight is full or not. Odds are that if they're asking for volunteers to take another flight, it's probably full. The best way to find out is to ask the agent when you check in, or an F/A when you board.

One of the biggest tips I can give you on getting spare seats is don't be the first to board. As a matter of fact, be one of the last. Flights will not leave earlier than their scheduled departure time. This way you can check out your seat and the people sitting around it; pass it by and see if there is a row empty, or a better seat. If there is, sit down as if it's yours. If someone comes to claim it, then just play dumb, excuse yourself, and move on. There is less likelihood that someone will claim it toward the end of boarding.

If you are already seated and have your eyes fixed on an empty row, odds are that ten other people also do. Just take the chance and move there. If you want to save yourself the embarrassment of being ejected from your seat, then you need to know when those spare seats are definitely not going to be utilized. The signal for that is when the ground agent or the chief purser makes the announcement "Will all ground staff please disembark," or "Flight attendants, prepare for departure." That is your signal that the door is, or is about to be, closed, and no further passengers will be boarding. All the spare seats in the respective classes are up for grabs. Sorry, no switching classes of service.

Unfortunately, with fares so competitive these days it's not as easy to get that much sought-after empty row or spare neighbor seat, especially on international flights. There are lucky exceptions, though, so good luck, and let the shuffling begin.

But one word of caution: if a F/A asks to use that empty seat or row next to you, please don't make a scene. After all, it's not actually your seat, but it was a good try.

Economy Class

BETTER KNOWN AS: COACH, Third Class, The Zoo, Thriftmart, Budget Barn, or, as everyone calls it now and then, The Jungle. It's the class where the seats are generally too small, meals are bland, cabins are usually overcrowded, you get treated like a third-class citizen, and perks are limited. A lot of the time you have no choice of meal except eat, or don't, and the wine selection is red or white. It's where the people who can't, or won't, pay the higher price for the more expensive classes. It's where you find the more casually dressed – sandals, shorts, tank tops, t-shirts – and the less deodorantly inclined.

Even so, the competition has grown fierce, and airlines are bidding for your business. There are bigger seats, better entertainment. Some airlines have video screens in every seat and video game playing capability. If they don't now, they will soon. There are also hot towels, free liquor, better-tasting and fairly substantial meals, and even an after-dinner liqueur service. All services that are offered on any one airline are, or will eventually be, offered on almost every other airline. The one exception to this is Virgin Airways. Some of Virgin's ideas include inflight gambling, massage, cosmetic consulting, tailoring, car shopping, etc. The list goes on, but no airline takes their ideas too seriously.

Amenities are definitely improving. Beyond the good and bad aspects, there is something that everyone is missing. It's the diversity of cultures. There are billions of people out there, and every one of them is different from the others in some way. If you can get over the look or the minor smell of the man next to you, he might come from the deepest part of Nepal and have lots to tell.

I once sat next to a man from Morocco, a woman from Vietnam, and a young girl from Iceland. We participated in a group discussion and learned a great deal about different views and ways of life. It's a crash course in cultural differences and the many pursuits of happiness. If you enjoy the person's company and would like to keep in touch, exchange addresses. If you don't care for this person, dislike or even despise them, just think, you will never have to see them again. Odds are that you won't.

I am what is called a "Coach-roach," a F/A who, even though I could work up in front, prefers to work in Economy. I find that it's where the most interesting people are. I am comfortable chatting, joking, and asking them questions about themselves. Yes, it can be quite a jungle, but at the end of the day I will have experienced many people's views, cultures, and excitement. Not like the "Wanna-Be's" in Business Class or the well-to-do in First. However, I am not suggesting for a moment that if you are offered an upgrade you should turn it down. That would be foolish – take it immediately, experience the differences, and enjoy.

I can't do anything about the seat comfort, and it seems that the airlines can't either. Unfortunately, there will usually be a crying baby in every section, but if you can tear yourself away from those distractions, you just might learn a little bit more about the world you're living in. Who knows, you might have a great time. Stranger things have happened.

Safety Dance

NICK WAS A MIDDLE-AGED man, but had always been afraid to fly. His job required him to do much traveling, so he devised a plan. He did some extensive research and concluded that out of all the seats on the airplane, and out of all the air disasters where some passengers survived, seat 34C was the safest. Through the years that was his seat, or nothing. He accrued so many frequent flyer points that he could be upgraded to First Class every time. He wouldn't have any of it. It was 34C or nothing. He even refused to fly once when they blocked off his seat because it was broken. He took the flight the following day. It was his superstition, and it worked for him.

He became quite a regular on my route, and I always looked forward to having him on my flights. He was the interesting type that I looked for in all passengers. Plenty of stories to tell, funny jokes, but we always ended up talking about this seat superstition. He told me that along with the statistics, he was 34 when he met his wife, his house address is 34, and his wife's bra size is, get this, 34C. So in his mind, fate for him is sitting in 34C. There was no arguing with that logic, I guess.

I was walking toward my flight when I heard an argument going on at the check-in desk. "I don't want an upgrade, I want to sit at 34C!"

I looked closer, and there he was having problems with an agent who wanted to upgrade a VIP of the frequent flyer program. "Hello, Nick," I waved. He smiled and waved back but was obviously tired of getting hassled about turning down upgrades.

In the end, he got his way and was assigned his famed seat, although this flight was not a great one for him. The light and movie audio were broken, only at that seat. A baby vomited on his shoes. A F/A spilled hot coffee in his lap, condensation dripped on his head, and the man in 34B had the worst case of body odor ever. He remained persistent in his belief that it was still his lucky seat. I made a point of looking after him the rest of the flight.

It was an especially hard landing, but only one overhead bin had opened. Can you guess which one? 34C. It shot open and a large suitcase landed directly on top of Nick. He was taken away by paramedics to be treated for a broken collarbone and a bruised spine.

Several months later, I walked through First Class and was shocked to see Nick.

"What are you doing up here?" I asked suspiciously.

He smiled at me, sipped his champagne, and replied, "I have modified my position on seats. 2B is my new choice. All that fate crap is for the birds."

Warning: if flying makes you nervous, I suggest you skip the rest of this chapter!

People often ask me where the safest place on the airplane is in an emergency. Well, to tell you the truth, since all accidents are different, it is an impossible question to answer accurately. All I can go on are the statistics that Nick told me. Many believe that it's up front, because it's by the cockpit, but statistics say no. Usually the First Class cabin is the first to go, along with the cockpit.

Most believe that the middle of the plane, over the wings, is the safest. The idea is that maybe the wings will absorb the shock and shelter you from obstacles such as trees, cars, etc. Right? Wrong again. This is one of the worst places. Each wing is carrying the fuel tanks which have 50% of the fuel, and if the tank blows up, so do you.

This leaves the very back. Yes, believe it or not, if you are in an accident and sitting in the back of the Economy section, your chances are the best for surviving. Therefore, while you don't get your choice of meals every time, you do have that knowledge to gnaw on. Unfortunately, I have to add that the odds, while greater than the ones up front, are still not very hopeful.

The safety video at the beginning of the flight mentions something about "in case of a water landing...." I have had passengers actually come up to me and ask if this flight was going to be a water landing or not. Just what is a water landing? Crew members call it "ditching,"a polite way of saying crashing into the water.

It is a last resort tactic used by the pilots. Sure, there are life rafts at every door, life jackets, and survival kits, but chances are that the plane will break apart into several pieces at first contact with the water. Meaning you'll probably never see the life rafts. The one apparatus that has the most chance of saving you is your life jacket, so listen next time the safety demo is played.

When I was in training, my safety instructor told us, "In the event of a ditching, you can kiss your ass good-bye! You are fish food, shark bait – in simpler terms, a goner!"

Not very encouraging words for a new hire. He went on to tell us about the glimmer of hope but, being a pilot, he didn't want to lie to us until we started flying.

He wasn't getting as many laughs as he expected, though I appreciated knowing the truth, rather than believing the fairy tale he was supposed to preach. Look at the environmental elements as well. You would last five minutes in the Atlantic, and then hypothermia would set in. There is very little information about water landings, because it hasn't happened very many times. So don't worry about it, because you have more of a chance of winning the lottery than being in a water landing or an air disaster.

If you are 50 times more at risk in an automobile than in an airplane, why are so many people afraid to fly? Is it because we are not in control of the plane like we are in a car? Maybe it's the fact that in a car, if we break down, we are not ten miles high in the sky in a metal tube. It could be due to the over-publicized and graphic details given through the media when an accident occurs. It could also have to do with the fear of heights that many share.

All flight attendants think about dying in an air disaster at one time or another. It is part of the job; they would be lying to you if they said they didn't. Their minds and hearts jump every time they, or their family, hear of a recent crash. For the first year, I couldn't stop dreaming about it. The dreams went from horrifying to kind of interesting.

I told my mother that if I died on a flight, I wished for my body to be cremated instead of buried. My mother smiled back and said that if I died on a flight, I wouldn't have much of a choice. We laughed morbidly, but profoundly. I don't have those crashing dreams anymore, but I do think about it – just about every flight.

Incidentally, if there is an air disaster and you are scheduled to fly within the next week, please don't joke about it with the crew. It is something we take very personally, and proper respect is due.

6

The Sky's the Limit

Not Every Question is a Good One

IT'S INTERESTING HOW PASSENGERS like to indulge in conversation with the flight crew, and vice versa. Usually, most of the passengers are on their way to a holiday destination, a family reunion, or maybe an exciting business excursion, and want to share the excitement. It makes time pass for both parties, and is, most of the time, well appreciated. There are a few questions that annoy us. Here are some to keep in mind:

We have just finished the service and are trying to eat our crew meals discreetly, when a passenger approaches, sees us, and says: "So, they let you eat too, huh?"

Now it doesn't sound that bad, but five seconds after that person leaves, another one arrives and says the exact same line. I actually count how many people ask me that each meal, and the holding record is 13. Usually by the fifth time, I lose my appetite. If you see food going in to our mouths, obviously we're not stealing it. They cater extra meals in First Class for more entree choices. The leftover entrees are the crew meals.

Also, while we are eating, please try not to peer into our food or watch us eat. It's bad enough that we have to eat standing up, much less constantly be watched. I respect your privacy, please respect mine.

Here's another one:

I am on an international flight from Los Angeles to Frankfurt, an 11-hour flight. A passenger comes up to me and asks, "Do you turn right around and go back to LA now?" Let's see, that would be 11-hour flight time x 2, plus four-hour airplane and cabin preparation for a grand total of 26 hours on duty?

No, we are only human. If you're saying to yourself that it is hard to believe that people actually ask that, it is the number one question.

"Have you ever been in a fatal airplane accident?"

Let's see. That would make me dead now, wouldn't it? I think the term "near fatal accident," or better yet, "close call" is what you're looking for.

"Do you get parachutes?"

At eight miles high in the sky with no oxygen, you would be dead before you reached the oxygen level.

"I'm never flying this airline again!"

If you've got to that point you have probably been a royal pain and all I'm thinking is, "Thank you!"

"Where are we now?"

Well, if we were over the Pacific Ocean 15 minutes ago and all you see is blue water, then chances are we're still over the Pacific Ocean.

"I could have your job for this!"

No, you can't, so don't flatter yourself.

"Do you know how much I paid for this ticket?!"

Listen, we don't care, and if you knew how much you should be paying, or what the fare is in First Class, you would retract that statement.

"Do you like working with so many beautiful women?"

Uh... no I prefer working with the ugly ones! What kind of question is that? Of course I do. It beats the military any day.

If a F/A comes through the aisles with a tray of glasses containing clear liquid with no bubbles, why does everyone automatically ask, "What is it?"

Well, it's certainly not vodka or gin!

To add to that, why do they ask us that with music or movie headphones on? You're just going to reply to my "Would you like some water?" with "What?" or the ever popular "Huh?"

"Water!"

"What?!!"

"WATER!"

You finally take off the earphones and scream, "What is it?!" for the fourth time, waking everyone around you, and then you say, "Uh, no thanks, can I have a coke?"

ARGH! NO!

Then I get to the next row that you have just woken, and they ask, "What is it?"

In the middle of a beverage service I get asked, "What do you have?"

My immediate thought is: I have 200 other people to serve who knows what the hell they want. But instead I tell him "Beer, wine, sodas, juices, mixed drinks, water, champagne, coffee, tea." To which the usual response is orange juice or coke. I push the cart one more row down, and, you got it, "What have you got?"

Hey, gang, take a chance. Call out what you want – we probably have it, and if not that, something close. My response to that question now is, "Everything, what would you like?"

"Orange juice."

To add on to that, when I get asked for a strawberry daiquiri, margarita, or pina colada, it really makes me chuckle. Do you see a blender on my cart?

I'm handing out newspapers on a Miami-London flight and somebody asks me for a *Denver Post* or a *Milwaukee Journal*. If we had a paper from each city in the USA, we wouldn't be able to fit any passengers on the flight, much less take off.

No, it's generally just the papers from origin and destination.

"Does it cost more to sit in First Class?"

Yes, that's the general idea.

Here are a couple of meal classics:

"How is that prepared?"
"Uh, well, it's heated up." The meals are already pre-cooked; all we do is heat them up. So I guess the answer is baked.

"What kind of chicken is that?"
What kinds of chicken are there?

Ok, last one, but one of my favorites.
We are still at the gate, and the passengers are stowing their bags. A woman comes up to me and says, "Can I go to the bathroom on the ground?"
"Uh, yes, ma'am, but we'd rather you use the toilets."

The Primal Scream

I FIND IT INTERESTING living with the full realization that each one of us has evolved through time. From caveman days of grunting, groaning, and battling with clubs, only to revert back when one steps foot on an aircraft. In a matter of 15 minutes, 12 people have come back to the rear galley to grunt and groan at me.

"Coffee!" he blurted out.

"What about coffee?" I inquired with an all-knowing grin.

"Do you have coffee?" he said in an annoyed tone.

"Yes I do, thank you." I replied, as I stared his way in anticipation.

"Well?"

"Well, what?"

"Can I have some?"

"Sure you can, Why didn't you just ask in the first place?"

"I thought I did," he mumbled, as he wandered away.

A lady entered the galley with an empty can and a used tissue stuffed halfway inside, motioning it my way, "Trash."

"Who are you calling trash?" I quipped

"No, not you, this is trash," she declared.

"Yes, it is, how wonderful."

"Do you have anywhere to put it?"

"Yes, I do."

"Where?"

"Right over there, thanks. Let me take it for you." She walked away wondering what got lost in the translation.

Where in the book of manners does it say common courtesy should be spared on airplanes? The sad thing is that nobody is actually trying to be rude. It's just the way the general public is trained.

A proper question, a "thank you," a "please," and a smile go a long way on an airplane – or anywhere, for that matter. But then again, this comes from a person who pushes a cart down the aisle screaming "BEEF or CHICKEN?"

Caviar Condiments

SAM REPORTED TO WORK that day feeling a little under the weather. His hay fever was running havoc with his sinuses, and he had the mother of all headaches. He was called in from reserve, so he was going to be the most junior, and probably assigned a position that nobody wanted. To his delight that position was the First Class aisle. This is normally the most senior position, but this time nobody wanted to work it due to the First Class galley chef (the one who prepares the meals and the carts). It was Helena the Horrible, so named by her peers.

Sam was a bit rusty with his First Class routine and serving techniques, but looked forward to the change of cabins. It was a full flight. The passengers did not look like they were going to be a fun crowd, but it was business as usual, hanging coats, offering pre-departure drinks, etc.

The plane took off and the F/As jumped into the service. Helena ordered Sam around, and he complied from a lack of experience. He served drinks as Helena prepared the carts for the service. Sam was determined to make this a successful flight. Everything he couldn't remember about the service, he just faked. He merely pretended to know what he was doing.

It came time for the meal. He set up the passengers' tray tables for dinner, repeating to himself, "Knives and spoons on the right, forks on the left."

He brought out the wines and bread rolls, practically running through the cabin. Not as easy as he thought.

"Young man! You had better save me a big portion of caviar," the obnoxiously snobbish woman by the window in the last row fluttered at him. She was the one who had thrown her fur coat at him during boarding.

"No problem, ma'am," he replied with a smile, but a scowl in his heart.

He went around with the appetizers, and when he reached the rude woman, she replied, "No, I'm saving myself for the caviar, thank you!"

Helena had the caviar cart ready by the time he had returned. "They only catered us with one can of caviar so that will have to last for everyone," Helena declared, totally disinterested.

Horror struck Sam. While he didn't particularly care about the snobby woman, he was new and did care about getting yelled at. One can was not going to be enough for 12 people.

Caviar condiments included egg whites, egg yolks, onions, sour cream, lemon, toast points, iced vodka or champagne. Maybe if he loaded the plates up with condiments they wouldn't miss the caviar. He thought about going to that woman first but knew she would ask for too much and there wouldn't be enough for everyone else, so he decided to ration, and just hope for the best. Some of the people didn't care for any, while others asked for more. He managed all right until he reached the passenger before the lady. There was a little bit more than one portion left as he muttered out his question.

"Would... would you like some caviar, sir?"

"Um, I've never had it before. Would I like it?" he quietly asked.

Normally Sam would have told him to try it, but this time he shook his head and whispered, "It's best you don't try it on an airplane. The first time I did, it made me ill."

The man declined gracefully, choosing iced vodka instead.

So far, so good, he thought as he rolled the cart beside the rude woman with folded arms and an 'about time' scowl on her face. She wanted all the condiments, so he went to work arranging them in a circular pattern and making the presentation perfect. He had the chopped onions in one hand and the plate in the other, when something horrible happened. He felt a tickle in his nose, and suddenly, in what seemed like slow motion, his hay fever let loose a big pool-like drop of mucus. He tried to turn away, but it was too late. He just had to hope for the best. The glistening stream headed straight for the... yep, you guessed it. A perfect shot, dead center, showered the caviar with a shiny new coat.

Horror-stricken, he stood perfectly still. His first thought was to run into the galley and get some more, but there wasn't any. The caviar was all gone. His second thought was to look at the woman to see if she had seen anything, so he could apologize. She hadn't, so he continued to look around to see if anyone had noticed. Slowly he stared each of the passengers straight in the eyes to see the slightest of grimaces or hints. There were none.

He looked back down at the woman. "Well, what are you waiting for?" she barked.

"Nothing, ma'am, sorry." He served up the now juicier looking morsel, presented it to her, and left in a hurry. Sam peeked from beyond the curtain several times to see if she had noticed something different. She hadn't, and continued to feast away on her salty fish egg delight. She practically licked the plate clean.

Sam finished the service with three tissues wedged up his nose, to prevent any further mishaps. He felt a twinge of guilt but, strangely enough, felt a small feeling of revenge as well.

Blue Genes

I WAS FLYING FROM Los Angeles to Munich one day in February. The holidays were over and work was routine. Out of the 100 passengers, nobody stood out. I always tried to make it a point to meet at least one interesting character each flight. All that there was to smile about today was the bright sun that I was unfortunately leaving behind.

An hour into the flight I spotted an odd-looking elderly man, about 70 years of age, with pure white hair down to his shoulders. He was dressed in blue jeans, a denim shirt, and had a heavy German accent. He was seated next to a sweet young girl who wasn't with him, but just a chance seat partner. She looked shy and very unsure of this man sitting beside her. He talked and laughed to himself a few times which made me unsure as well, so I asked her discreetly if she wanted to move, in order to lessen an uncomfortable situation. She declined, politely, not wishing to cause a scene. The man just sat staring straight ahead, with a kind but goofy grin fixed on his face.

The flight pushed on, and I hadn't heard or seen a trace of him until a couple of hours later when a guttural laugh pierced my eardrums. The odd gentleman was talking to a fellow flight attendant about the closing of the Berlin Wall. It turned out that he had been there the day it came down, which was a coincidence, because I, too, was there on a layover on that historic day. So I joined the conversation, and we ended up talking for hours, laughing and commenting on the different aspects of the Wall and how it had affected everyone's lives.

His name was Gunther, 78 years old, from Berlin, a retired

physicist who was returning from hiking with his son in the mountains. There was something vaguely familiar about him. I searched my mind, and then it hit me. He was the mirror image of Albert Einstein, all except for the blue jeans and the hiking boots.

"Has anyone ever told you that you look just like...."

"Ya, ya, Albert Einstein. I get zis remark quite often," he interrupted. "Funny sing is, I didn't use his theories for most of my career." We laughed on.

If you look at it, a German physicist, long white hair, in his seventies. It was Einstein, or the closest thing to him that I would ever meet.

He was a kind old man, and talking with him, quite frankly, made my flight. This made me somewhat ashamed of my first assessment, but looks can and often do deceive. I could see the sparkle in his eyes as he spoke, but then again, perhaps it was the relief of someone finally talking to him once during the 12-hour flight.

I went to his seat at the end of the flight, shook his hand, and said my German farewells. He handed me a piece of paper with his name and address in Berlin, and told me that if I was ever in town to please stop by and see him. I thanked him and promised him I would (which, this time, I really meant). Meanwhile, the young girl next to him wondered about the transformation in my hospitality.

Three months later, my work took me to Berlin for a 24-hour layover. I called Gunther to try to arrange a meeting. His daughter answered and said he had passed away a couple of months before – a mere one week after he returned from his trip to California. I told her that I was very sorry to hear the news, but that I was a better person for knowing him. Which I was.

May you rest in peace, Gunther, $E=MC^2$.

What's the Matter With Harry?

THIS STORY HAS A twist. It runs like the river...on and on it flows by its own momentum. Like the river, addiction goes on forever; we don't know where it starts, and we don't know where it ends. It just is. The river, like addiction, is sometimes calm on a warm and sunny day. Other times, it rages with storm, if fueled by even just a little rain.

Harry knew the storm; Harry knew the rain. Appearing to be about 60 years old, he had deeply carved lines around his eyes. There were hues of blue and gray that deepened if he tried to smile because the smile never reached his blank eyes. With a strong Irish accent, he roamed around the airplane, seemingly unsure of why he was there. The one thing he was sure of was that he wanted alcohol, and at regular intervals. As I gazed at him gulping down his gin with barely a breath between gulps, I suspected that he might have lost something or someone. His hunger yearned on and played havoc with his heaving frame. If you looked at him, even from afar, you could actually feel the tremble, the hunger, the dark need.

At first, because I didn't think he was hurting anyone, I fed him his requested doses, until the classic signs told me to slow him down. I began to see the mental deceleration, the melting that happens when too much cloudiness takes over the brain, and the fog rolls in. The final clincher was when another elderly man came over and pointed out Harry as his brother, and told us not to let him have any alcohol because he had a severe drinking problem.

OOPS. " Uh...we've just cut him off, sir," I sheepishly replied.

He frowned with embarrassment and told me Harry's story. They had both been in New Zealand where Harry's son was getting married. Halfway through the reception, they had been asked to leave, due to Harry's lack of control. In other words, he was bombed the entire time and was a major embarrassment. His brother, who hadn't seen him in quite a number of years, was shocked to discover the severity of his problem. He pleaded for us not to give his little brother one more drop.

"Don't worry, we weren't going to anyway. Did you say little?" Harry was not a small man, and must have weighed over 225 pounds. He looked quite a few years older than his brother.

"Yes, Harry is 45 years old, I'm 61."

I kept my next comment to myself but considered becoming a teetotaler immediately.

Harry kept coming back and asking for a drink, but my answer was the same. He returned to his seat each time like a punished puppy dog. This happened no less than eight times. Every time he came up to me with such great hope, I could actually feel his addiction, to the point that I began to need a stiff drink myself. A few minutes later, I heard a loud thud coming from the lavatory. I knocked and entered, only to catch Harry swigging or, I should say, chugging from a Scotch bottle that he had bought from duty-free. I grabbed the bottle, scolded him, and confiscated his liquor. His brother came back, and they argued a bit. Ten minutes later, I caught him up in Business Class, asking for a drink there.

I can only guess that he was on a suicide mission. The alcohol numbed his emotions, and when some inkling of feeling returned, it was time for more anesthetics. I couldn't begin to imagine the embarrassment of being told to leave your own son's wedding. I could just about hear his liver screaming, as he returned once more.

"Gin, please," Harry said with a smile. I actually think he believed he would be served.

"You don't seem to understand that you are not going to be served any more liquor for the rest of the flight," I replied sternly.

"Yeah, but that was a long time ago. I just want one," he begged with sad eyes.

"It's not gonna happen; you are officially cut off. How about some orange juice?"

"No, thank you," he said as he returned to his seat on the verge of tears.

He eventually passed out, and we landed without further incident. Returning home after the flight, I indulged in a tall glass of Scotch and toasted poor old Harry.

I felt I needed it ...(uh oh).

The Witching Hour

IT'S THE POINT OF non-compliance – in one ear and out of the other, eight hours down and too many to go, tired, sweaty, nod your head to anything, pretend to listen to your concerns, etc. Yes, folks, welcome to the infamous and traditional "I JUST DON'T CARE HOUR."

It usually occurs on those full-load-that-nothing-goes-right flights. The ones where everyone has missed their connections and blames us, and tells us of their woes. We may be smiling, but there is nobody home. Some disguise it better than others do, and others deny that they ever reach it. We all do at one time or another, and when we do, there will be little or no sincere sympathy or emotion released.

Our main objective, at that point, is to get you off that plane without saying something that we might regret. It's the time we fear our own dark sides. Everyone has different releases for the frustration associated with the phenomenon. Some drink heavily after the flight, others seek their revenge on specific troublemakers during the flight, but most just make fun of certain passengers back in the galley. Luckily, I have a fun, fairly humorous method – I joke.

I joke with the guy when he tells me that the food was terrible. "You should have been here on mystery meat day!"

I joke with the guy after he throws up all over the floor in the galley. "We never served you carrots."

Or with the lady who tells me that such-and-such airline is better. "It's probably true, but why are you here?"

"I'm never flying with this airline again!!"

"Oh, that's what you said last time."

I could tell you what an ugly baby you have, and the way I say it will have you in laughing hysterics.

Marathoners hit the wall, housewives reach the breaking point, business men and women get to the edge, and so do flight attendants. It's not a violent thing, it's just an "I don't care" time.

If you ask directions from someone in that state of mind, it would behoove you to double-check the information, for it might be one of our revenge tactics, or we are just too fed up to say "I don't know." When you recognize a crew member who has reached this stage, go to a different one, because you won't get anywhere beating that dead horse.

A Very Special Brew

AN OLDER LADY AROUND 65 boarded the overcrowded flight from Europe carrying a golden vase. It struck me as quite odd, until I realized that it was an urn. I went to her seat to see if I could help or comfort her. She was very nice, but declined. I glanced at the seat next to her and noticed the urn had a seat belt strapped around the handles.

"It's my husband – he died while we were in Germany. We knew it was going to happen, but didn't know when." She continued, "If you're wondering why he's in the seat, it's a non-refundable ticket. Instead of having someone crowding me, I have my own space."
She had a sweet smile and a firm grasp on the situation. She was right – they wouldn't have given her a refund and would have stuck someone else in the seat next to her. It was a good idea.

It was a full flight and that seat was the only empty one. Well, technically empty. I liked her immediately, and decided to check on her from time to time. About midway through the flight, I went over to her for a chat. She told me that this was the first flight ever that she couldn't sleep. I told her that it was understandable considering what had taken place.

She went on to explain that they had had a wonderful life together, and it had been a beautiful trip until he died. One moment he was eating schnitzel, drinking beer, and laughing. The next moment he was gone. I told her that it sounded like a great way to go. We both chuckled a bit. I offered some champagne from First Class, but she opted for a cup of hot water instead. I complied and went back to work.

I glanced up the aisle minutes later to see her opening the urn. Horror struck seconds later as I evaluated and then dismissed certain thoughts. Just in case, I decided to investigate. I returned to where she was seated and caught her spooning some of her husband's ashes into her cup.

She looked up in embarrassment and replied, "I know it looks funny, but I feel that it is a way of having a tiny bit of him inside of me. Especially poignant at the high altitude we're flying at, closer to heaven and all."

I didn't stop her. I told her that it probably wasn't very good for her, but she didn't care. Her reasoning behind it made some sense, and even if I'd wanted to, I didn't think I had a right to stop her.

It was a strange tribute, but wonderful. I just hope it didn't make her ill.

7

Working the Aisles

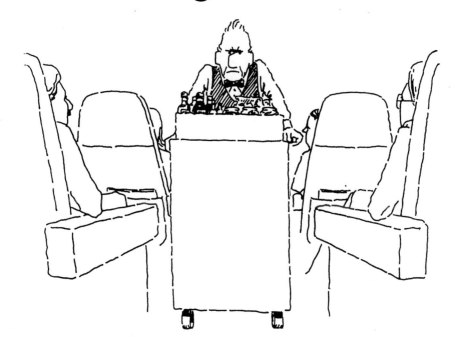

Taming of the Stew

EVERYONE IN THIS LIFE has their little pet peeves, even flight attendants. The problem is that these annoyances may seem innocent, and the average passenger may be unaware of the irritating result. The following is a short list of actions that may enrage your F/A.

1. Press your F/A call button on, then off, repeatedly. It will send a tone into the galley that will drive us mad after a while.

2. Tap us on any part of the body, or snap your fingers to get our attention.

3. Pile the dishes and trash on your meal tray in such a way that when it is collected, everything falls all over the floor. Then sneer at us as if it is our fault.

4. Ask several different F/As for the same thing.

5. Talk to us with your mouth full, thus showering us with your food and spittle.

6. Come back to our galley and pass gas or be sick.

7. Let your kids run around unattended.

8. Ask for three or more drinks at a time.

9. Take a bite out of your meal and reconsider entree choices.

10. Combine two or more meal trays together after you're finished eating. It may seem like you're helping, but the stacked tray won't fit back into the cart, so we have to re-stack them. However, thank you for the thought.

11. Stick your leg out in the aisle and then threaten a lawsuit when we hit it with the meal cart.

12. Tell us in detail how badly the airline has inconvenienced you.

13. Insist on getting up when the seatbelt sign is turned on. Do you think we actually get some kind of pleasure telling you to return to your seat? We do it for your safety and those around you and, most importantly, because those are the rules. If it were up to me, I would just let you take your chances. I feel that the seatbelt sign is warning enough. If you had seen your fellow colleague break her neck on the ceiling panel as I have, you would reconsider that bathroom stop or drink venture.

14. Sit or walk around in a cabin that's a higher class than the one that you're assigned. It's not even worth the try, and you end up looking foolish when the F/A asks you to return to your section.

15. Hand us your warm and gushy sick bag or diaper.

The Cockpit Cruise

COCKPIT CREWS ARE A SOMETIMES interesting but oftentimes boring breed. The stereotypical pilot is a cheap, macho, girl-in-each port, vain guy named Bob. You would be surprised how many of the cockpit crew actually fit that description, although it's not fair to generalize because, according to the typical male flight attendant stereotype, I should be a thin, gay, immaculately groomed, effeminate guy named Bruce. These are the men and women whom we entrust with our lives each time we board an airplane. They go through intensive training and safety checks all the time to keep you safe. From a distance, they command a certain amount of respect, but up close, some lose it quickly. How about the pilot who got arrested for driving under the influence? He was two times over his limit, in uniform and on his way to a 747 flight. Or the pilot who was served 14 rum-and-cokes in the cockpit? There is a pilot whom I fly with who covers himself up in wet linens when he flies (head to toe), to avoid polar radiation. We refer to him as "Mummy Dearest."

It may be a non-smoking flight, but that doesn't mean they're not smoking up in the cockpit. Next time you fly, watch and see who gets off first. It should be the passengers, but stand clear of the commuting pilot.

These days, an airplane doesn't only have the capability to fly on its own, but it can also take off and land by computer. What do we need a cockpit crew for? I'd like to see how many tickets are sold without them.

Female F/As typically claim they don't date the guys in the cockpit, but if they do, they won't admit it until it gets serious. In the cockpit they are guilty (promiscuous) until proven innocent (trustworthy). Fair enough, they assume I'm gay until told differently. Not that it would make any difference, but the cockpit is still fairly uncomfortable with the gay persuasion.

The cockpit and F/As are not at war, but they both know that they are each looking out for their own kind. Next time you see a pilot on break, admire his First Class seat, then notice the F/As' Economy rest seats. I remember a certain pilot who was upset about only receiving a $1 million early retirement offer. F/As would be lucky to see 4% of that.

As a child, my dream was to be a commercial airline pilot until, heartbroken, I discovered that partial color blindness was a disqualifier. I didn't set out then to become a flight attendant, it just happened. Now that I have layovers with pilots in places all around the world, I find them somewhat disappointing. They never want to explore or go on an adventure, while the flight attendants continually go on safaris, rainforest tours, jungle trekking, you name it.

I have never met an occupation that earns so much, but spends so little (some call it thrifty, I call it cheap). A pilot's typical first remark is "How much?" They would rather eat at the hotel restaurant than out in the layover city where the real people are. I know a few pilots who are proud when they do not leave the hotel once in a four-day layover in India. That's an accomplishment to be proud of?

My wife is currently making the transition from flight attendant to pilot and now I can understand some of their habits better. They are cheap because they have had to pay so much to get to where they are. It's instinctual to look for the free food, happy hours, and the good deals. They are virtually broke while they are paying for their training and building hours to get on with the airlines. Either that or they have multiple alimony payments to pay.

Times are definitely changing up in the front. As the pilots have a mandatory retirement at 60, a younger breed is coming in. I walked into the cockpit on a flight awhile back and greeted them with a "hi guys," and two young ladies turned around and smiled. Now, in no way do I consider myself sexist, but the role reversal was hard for me at first. Of course, I got used to it, and now it's a pleasant change. Even the name "cockpit" has been officially changed to the more politically correct "Flight Deck."

Along with the new breed of pilots comes a new prospective

relationship between the two occupations. Pilots are actually given a class on how to get along with the F/As, and vice versa. With mandatory alcohol and drug testing now in force, past security indiscretions that I mentioned earlier have been mostly eliminated. I can proudly say that my airline has some of the best-trained pilots in the world, and that gives me confidence whenever I fly.

Here are a few classic cockpit jokes. Please realize that it's all in good fun.

> *What separates the scum of the earth from the rest of the world?*
> The cockpit door.

> *Did you hear about the captain who took his wife out to dinner and a movie?*
> The flight canceled. (cheap)

> *What does a pilot use for birth control?*
> His personality.

> *What does he use for back up?*
> His layover clothes.

> *What's the difference between the cockpit and a porcupine?*
> The porcupine has the pricks on the outside.

> *What's the difference between the cockpit and a condom?*
> You can only get one dick into a condom.

Okay to be fair:

> *What do you call a bunch of flight attendants in a basement?*
> A wine cellar.

There are many more about F/As but let a pilot tell you those.

One more thing: several people have asked me about how I will feel if my wife is hired as a pilot with the same airline as the one I work for as a flight attendant. I have no problem with that, ego-wise, and I welcome the extra money as well. But I can tell you, if we work the same flight some day... she can get her own damn coffee!

Spin It

IT WAS THE CREW from hell; the melting pot with way too much heat. Hilda was a 40-year veteran with a "the-company-screwed-me" attitude. Bruce was an overtly gay man who was sure Ron was a homophobic bigot. Ron was a straight F/A who looked in the mirror at every chance and was sure that Bruce was hitting on him. Yolanda was a thirties-something black lady who had her suspicions that Mary was a racist. Mary was a heavily accented woman from South Carolina who sported a prissy attitude to everyone. Betsy was a 19-year-old F/A on her first flight ever and was so nervous that she kept dropping everything. The cockpit was void of all personality. I was a newly transferred F/A assigned to this flight as the purser and dreading the ten-hour flight in front of us.

Heavy bickering went on between all of us for the first three hours, but after that the silent treatment prevailed. That's when you know everyone truly dislikes one another; nobody tries to work things out. Luckily the passengers were nice, so no incidents occurred, but the hours limped along in a slow, torturous way. A 50-hour layover in Los Angeles and sunning on the beach was the only thought keeping us from strangling one another.

We checked into the hotel and everyone disappeared to their rooms. I was not surprised in the least when nobody made plans to meet up for dinner or drinks. The weather turned out to be dire and flash flood warnings were in effect for the whole coastal area. The rain was coming down so hard that leaving the hotel was next to impossible. I was lucky because my room was a suite with a large living room and bar. Normally, if a crew member got a suite he or she would host a layover party, but I cringed at the thought of this crew getting together. I toyed with the idea for a while and out of pure boredom, I wrote up some notes inviting anyone stranded in their rooms to a get-together. A flood party if you will. I put the notes under their doors and hoped for the worse.

So there I sat, with a twelve-pack of beer on ice, chips and dip and a cigar for when nobody showed up. Was I crazy? Did I really want to see these people on my off time? After an hour alone I opened a beer and reached for the lighter. To my surprise, I heard a knock on the door. It was Betsy and Ron.

"Is your party still going on?" Ron asked.

"Actually, we're it," I replied.

One by one, people showed up until everyone from the crew arrived. Even Bob, one of the younger pilots, showed up. It was quiet and awkward until Hilda brought out her body flask full of vodka. It contained at least a liter and had obviously been taken off the airplane.

"It's allowed in the contract under the Old Bag clause," she smirked.

Everyone laughed, apart from Betsy, who was wondering if there really was such a clause. We made up a batch of strong Bloody Marys and people started to loosen up and talk to each other. Betsy got tipsy after two sips and suggested we play "Spin the Bottle." Some scoffed at the juvenile suggestion and others shrugged it off like they didn't know what it was.

"You know, truth or dare! I spin the bottle, and whomever it lands on has to say 'truth or dare'. If they say 'truth', the spinner asks them a personal question. If they say 'dare', the spinner dares them to do something embarrassing."

"We're not in high school anymore, honey," Bruce snickered.

"What the hell, I'm in," Hilda announced.

Everyone topped up their drink and gathered around the coffee table. Betsy spun the empty beer bottle and it landed on Hilda.

"I better start out with a truth," she replied.

"Where is the strangest place you ever kissed a man?" Betsy asked.

"Um, I don't know." Hilda paused. "I guess, on the bottom."

The whole room roared with laughter at the misunderstanding. The liquor flowed faster and the game got more interesting. Hilda spun and it landed on Bruce.

"Have you ever slept with a woman?" The whole room deadened with silence for an answer.

"Oh yeah, but I quickly went off seafood."

The laughter became contagious. The truths ran their course, during which the following was revealed:

Mary was not a racist but engaged to a black man. Yolanda used to be a stripper. Ron was in love with himself. Bob was a member of the Mile High Club, and Betsy was "technically" a virgin.

"Dare!" Hilda declared.

The room silenced as this was the first dare of the evening and it was my turn to ask. I thought about it for a while and decided to start the dares with a tame one.

"Take out and show us the most embarrassing item in your purse." I was expecting a bad photograph or something similar.

She searched her purse and paused for a second. "Are you sure? Ah, what the hell." She brought out a small silk bag, opened it, and placed a vibrator on the table. A short silence and then the room exploded in laughter.

Betsy laughed along with the crowd but then asked, "What is it?"

Everyone laughed harder as Hilda reached down and turned it on. Betsy turned bright red as the contraption buzzed around the table. It took a good 15 minutes for everyone to recover from the hysterics. Hilda had started a trend, so everyone had to attempt a dare. Yolanda performed a lap dance on Bruce. I had to kiss Betsy in a convincing manner. Mary ran down the hall dressed only in a washcloth. Halfway she ran into a Japanese pilot crew going to their rooms. They were all smiles.

Then it came to Ron. Betsy had no clue on what to dare him, so she asked for suggestions.

"Show us the goods!" shouted Hilda.

Everyone laughed but shrugged it off as unfair. Ron insisted he was more than happy to do it. He was a bragger, so obviously he had something to show. He took down his pants and to everyone's amazement, it was, let's just say, extremely short of expectations. Once again, the room exploded with laughter.

"I guess I should have thought that one through a little more," Ron declared.

The evening ended with aching stomachs from the excessive laughter. Everyone had a great time.

We had the best flight home and parted what appeared as the best of friends. Many different vehicles can bridge gaps. This one, "Spin The Bottle," seemed to close the generation, race, and gender gap. Potential enemies laughed with instead of at one another. In this world, we all take great comfort in the fact that we are different from one another; however, we should take that same comfort in our similarities.

Next time you are at an awkward gathering and seeking a solution, don't automatically dismiss the silly juvenile suggestions. Why not put a spin on the scene?

Gotcha

DO YOU EVER WONDER why F/As occasionally break out in laughter during the safety demonstration? No, we don't consider the demo a particularly funny thing to watch, either. What you don't realize is that as you sit staring straight ahead at the F/A, they are staring at their colleagues standing in the back of the cabin, who are probably acting in some obscene or moronic manner to get the F/A facing you to laugh or to leave his or her position in hysterics. They are playing a game of "Gotcha." The F/As facing you win if they can keep a straight face. A smile is considered a draw, and a laugh or leaving the demo position is a loss. If they don't look, then it's considered chickening out, and is also not very sporting.

Next time they laugh, look down the aisle but prepare yourself. I have seen it all, and some of it's not a pretty sight. I have seen people strip, pour milk all over themselves, wear wigs, or throw a moon (expose their butt). I have even seen a mock orgy.

Now, I know what you're probably thinking: how juvenile, right? Yes it is, but at the same time, it's a release, a way of laughing at ourselves. You might think that we should be watching the safety video instead of playing a game. Listen, we know the safety demo by heart. I think I have even dreamed about it several times.

I can remember one time when I got into my demo position awhile back. I knew that I was in trouble, because the wildest F/A at the base was on my trip. She and I were avid Gotcha players. I was determined not to react. I wanted this win. She started with mild stuff, but it had no effect on me. It was as she hiked up her skirt and disclosed a full wig of hair lodged between her legs, that I started to weaken. I thought of everything depressing I could muster and repeated "dead puppies, dead puppies" over and over in my mind. I was going to win.

She got frustrated and surrendered by going into the toilet. I was quite proud of myself, when all of a sudden she emerged from the toilet stark naked, wearing nothing but sanitary napkins on the important bits. I totally lost it, and unfortunately the game. She was declared the Gotcha champion.

A couple of months later, I started dating a girl at my base named Martha. We had been seeing quite a bit of each other, and had been working the same trips. One flight, when she and her best friend were at the demo positions, I deemed it a perfect opportunity to give them both an induction to the Gotcha game. I went into my routine, sanitary napkins, stripping, acrobatics, the works. Martha left her spot, and her friend didn't stop laughing. They were easy targets. I declared victory and left it at that.

Well, the joke backfired. Apparently there was an FAA inspector (Federal Aviation Administration – the safety police), on board, and he wrote me up on formal charges for interfering with safety matters. OOPS!

I received my official letter of charge a month later, the day Martha and I were working a trip to Europe. Up to that point, all I could think about was a romantic layover, but when I opened the letter, all I could do was fear the worst. It was from the FAA stating that on such and such date I was observed interfering with the safety demonstration on such and such flight, which violates such and such code of conduct, etc. The letter went on for three more pages and ended with "a hearing will be scheduled within the next two weeks, pending suspension and/or discharge."

Oh shit! I was in trouble. They had me dead to rights. My whole job passed in front of my eyes. What was supposed to be a trip of romance might end up as my last flight. Fear struck hard, for it was true, the charges were accurate. I was guilty. What was I going to do? Thoughts of moving back home, reapplying at college, trying to get my bartending job back, passed through my mind. I had never been fired from a job before. I had yet to see certain parts of the world with this job, and now I was going to have to pay for the airline tickets! My heart sank as I read the letter a second time.

"What's wrong?" Martha asked trying to read over my shoulder.

"Huh? Uhm, nothing," I replied, trying to appear cocky.

I would fight it. That's what I'd do. I would state that I was never in that vicinity of that part of the aircraft. Martha and her best friend would be my witness. It would be three against one.

"Do you want to get some coffee before briefing?" Martha suggested.

"Uh, no, I've got to do some work on the computer before we go." I smiled and gave her a wink. I walked straight past the computers and into my supervisor's office. I showed her the letter and stated how ridiculous this accusation was and how furious I was at this letter. My fear turned into anger as I created alibis, witnesses, and lied through my teeth, and I did it quite masterfully, I might add. She was as shocked as I was that she hadn't been notified of it first. All complaints usually go through the F/A's supervisor first. She vowed to fight it with me.

In the heat of the discussion Martha walked by appearing a bit nervous. She poked her head in and said "I'm sorry to interrupt, but can I speak to you?"

"I'm a bit busy right now. I'll be out in a second," I replied, in a somewhat annoyed tone.

A couple of seconds later, she re-emerged and this time my supervisor was getting annoyed. "Once again, I'm sorry, but please do me a favor and read the signature at the end of the letter." Martha closed the door and left for briefing.

What? I was confused. What was she talking about? I scanned the FAA letter to the signature and it read,

> Sincerely Yours,
> G. Otcha
> FAA Inspector # 10SNE1

My body and mind sank in disbelief. G Otcha. Gotcha! This was a payback of the worst kind. Martha had gotten me as I had never been gotten before. I apologized to my supervisor, who thought that it was quite funny. I was lucky she had a sense of humor (most supervisors don't).

I went into the flight briefing in a daze, and was greeted by a round of applause by the entire crew who had been told the whole story. I walked in, went over to Martha, got down on one knee and declared, "I officially announce: you have gotten me like no one ever before. You are my champion! Congratulations." Then I kissed her.

I was a good sport, and my feelings for her rose a couple of notches. I have to admit that it took several hours, if not the whole flight, to get over the shock of the emotional roller coaster that I had just been through. I never played the Gotcha game again. Just in case you were wondering, I eventually married my champion, and have the infamous letter framed and mounted in our house.

Seniority

SENIORITY.... IT'S AS PRECIOUS as gold, and the backbone to all flying. It is what all decisions are based on. It has the final word. It can make or break the F/A job, your life and attitude. Mess with a F/A's seniority, and watch a kind and pleasant person turn into a fire-breathing dragon.

Once a flight attendant is hired, he or she is given a specific number on the basis of the date of hire. From that moment on, any F/A hired afterward is deemed "more junior," everyone before, "more senior." The more senior you are, the more options you have. Options such as trips, working days, off time, vacation, work positions, trades, and even hotel room selection.

Conversely, the more junior you are, the less options you have. You get what the more senior ones don't want. If you are really junior, then you could be on reserve and have no options at all. A F/A will be sorry to see a friend transfer to another base, but if her friend was more senior than she was, she secretly smiles as she bids her a fond farewell.

Mergers happen quite frequently – when they do, the merging F/As have a right to seniority based on their date of hire. Oh, the feathers that get ruffled here.

"Why should they get seniority just because they were with a shitty airline?"

It does get vicious. Seniority can range from the most senior at 50 years of service to one day. That's a half a century of seniority and, believe me, every day has value.

Furloughs and redundancies (layoffs) are also done on a seniority basis. It might be at a base of 5,000 F/As, but senior staff make it their business to know who is more junior and senior to them. Some bases have what F/As call "Seniority Watch." This is a group who watches the retirements and obituaries of the more senior each month.

"Oh, Mary Dobbs died last week of cancer."

"How terrible!" Now, what she's thinking deep down is, "Was she more senior than me?"

It may sound morbid, but it's true.

A Gray Matter

HOW MANY TIMES HAVE you boarded a flight and discovered that the elderly lady you were about to help to her seat was one of the flight attendants on your trip that day? Wait a minute, what ever happened to "Fly Me" or "Coffee, Tea or Me"? It's more like "Help Me" or "Coffee, Tea or Geritol." It's not like the typecast stewardess – the lovely young women always looking for that pilot to settle down with. This is real life. These are the women who turned a part-time, single, young female-type job into a lifelong career.

If you happen to board a flight that has primarily older female F/As on it, it is probably a flight that is worth a lot of hours, not too much work, or headed to a popular destination.

Why are some of the F/As so elderly and still working? There is currently no age limit, thanks to the Age Discrimination in Employment Act. So those young "Fly Me" girls of yesterday are still flying and enjoying a career. The only test of ability comes with a safety refresher course each year. They have to be able to open a door in a mock evacuation and complete a simple written test.

There is no real reason for them to retire. They get the equivalent of three months paid vacation each year. They get to fly free, and it gives them something to do. Remember, we can fly as much or as little as we want (provided we can get someone to cover our minimum hours). The senior F/As get the better trips.

There are many reasons the older crew members stay on. Besides the personal reasons, one of the main reasons is that the airline doesn't provide them with a proper retirement plan. Most airlines don't even contribute a percentage to a 401(k) retirement plan as most big businesses do. Why? Perhaps the airlines didn't plan on the flight attendant job as a career, or maybe they didn't count on these ladies lasting this long? No, I am sorry to say, the reason is that the airlines are just too cheap. It returns to haunt them, because one senior F/A gets paid the same as two and a half new-hire F/As.

Yes, the older F/As bring wisdom and expertise to the job, but they also get paid twice as much. The main point is that two for the price of one is a harsh reality for the airlines.

While I am proud of these senior F/As, the age maximum is getting a bit out of control. There is a lady based in Atlanta who is 77 years old and still flying as a flight attendant. She looks as though she needs the cart in the aisle to hold her up. While people may think that it's cute, is this one of the people who is going to save your life in an emergency? Somehow, I think not.

There also was a 66-year old flight attendant from San Francisco who died while working a flight. It happened during take-off. She was discovered a half an hour later still strapped to her seat. It was determined that she died of natural causes, which is a bit frightening. This incident is somewhat sad because her flying partners applied for understaffing pay, because a replacement wasn't provided. Ahh, respect for the dead! The other F/As were fully entitled to it, and I'm sure the deceased F/A would have wanted it that way.

I have flown with a lot of older ladies and found many of them extremely pleasant and fun to work with. Then there are the ones that are bitter and try to make it difficult for the younger F/As. They often speak about the 'good old days' and how so-and-so working in Economy crossed the picket line in 1955. They never forget who the scabs are. Many are just plain irritated that they are at retirement age and can't afford to quit. They often try to deflate a new hire's excitement on the job.

How nice or bitter they are makes no difference. There are generalizations in every facet of life. However, there is a growing consensus that there should be a mandatory retirement age of 65. The pilots have to retire at 60, and flight attendants are in an equally demanding safety-related profession.

The fact of the matter is that a F/A's job is considered a career for many. Both sides, management and flight attendants, need to meet halfway and decide on a mandatory retirement age, with a better retirement system. The way things stand now, if F/As retire, they feel like they are surrendering, and management has won, so they hang on as long as they possibly can. Everyone is supposed to enjoy the "golden years," not fight their way through them.

Joe Public

THERE ARE SO MANY different flight attendants flying out of different bases that it is feasible to fly with new faces for an entire career. Occasionally, one stands out that you never quite forget.

I met Danny on a trip to Vancouver. He was 36, happily married, and had an eight-year-old son. What stood out about him was his fun-loving demeanor and wicked sense of humor. Chicken was our only meal choice; however, he would offer chicken or possum. In the unlikely event that they chose the possum, he would hand them our only choice and warn them that it tasted like chicken. He flirted with the older ladies, played with the children, and was a great joy to work with.

During deplaning an elderly gentleman approached and complimented him on a wonderful landing.

"No, sir, I'm not the pilot, just a flight attendant," he replied.

Danny paused, then turned to me with a stern look on his face. "Frank, the next time I say that, I will quit."

"Don't sweat it; I say that by mistake once in a while myself."

"It really gets to me. I promise you, next time I will quit!" he said while getting his jacket on.

Danny was a regular to Vancouver, so I agreed to go to his favorite Irish pub. I was soon to find out that my new fun-loving friend was in the middle of a mild mid-life crisis. After a few pints of beer, the conversation began to roll. Danny had only worked in the service industry. He had been a busboy while in elementary school and a waiter through high school, and had worked his way through college as a bartender. He decided that he would become a flight attendant for a couple of years and see the world. Thirteen years and millions of miles later, he was still at it. (A story known by many in this job.)

Danny had a wife who made double his salary, in-laws who were disgusted with his occupation, and parents who were disappointed that he had never utilized his degree. Now, he was demeaning himself by telling the public that he was "just a flight attendant."

"I found out that my son didn't invite me to career day because he lied to all his friends and told them that I was a pilot," he downed the rest of his beer and ordered another round. "So the easy solution to my dilemma is to quit, right? The kicker to this whole story is that I love my job. Life is exciting. I get to see my kid grow up. I love my wife. I don't battle with daily traffic, and I live life a little easier than the normal Joe Public. I would hate to be him."

I didn't have the answers for him because many of his issues were alive in me at the time. Misery loved company that night, and one too many beers were consumed.

I didn't see or hear anything from Danny until several months later. I heard that he quit in the middle of a flight. I just assumed that he followed through with his promise and quit. I silently wished him well, for life after the airline world is an uncertain one.

Several months later, I got a surprise call from Danny.

"Yeah, I said it again and quit. I got a so-called break and went to work for an insurance agency. My wife wasn't used to having me around all the time and eventually left me. I hate my job. I got pulled over for drunken driving, but besides that life is just grand."

"I am sorry to hear it, buddy. Things will get better for you. You're in the adjustment period. You'll see." It was my best advice from the top of my head.

"Yeah, I hope so. Hey, the reason I am calling you is I was wondering if you still wrote those little story articles?"

"Sure, why?"

"Well, I thought maybe you could write one about my situation. Advise fellow flight attendants not to do anything rash when it comes to quitting. The grass isn't greener on the other side, and being Joe Public isn't all that it's cracked up to be."

I told him that I would see what I could do, and we made plans to meet up for golf sometime in the spring. Plans that eventually faded from both of our memories.

Two years later, I received word that Danny had killed himself. He swallowed a bottle of sleeping pills and chased it with a pint of vodka. A note was found next to him that read, "I'm outta here."

I felt extremely guilty that I hadn't reached out and done more for him. He wasn't a close friend, just a fellow worker on a layover in Canada. Nevertheless, I feel as if in some way I let him down. I can't say why he took his life, but we can all learn an invaluable lesson from his story. Danny let others dictate his life. He didn't know what he wanted; however, he did know what he didn't want to become, and became it anyway. He turned into the very person he claimed to loathe that night in Vancouver.

Don't let anybody tell you how to, or how not to, live your life. You hold the key to your own happiness, and it is up to you to find that key. Life is too short to live up to the expectations of others, or to suffer through a job that you hate.

Danny, thank you, and I'm sorry.

Pranks and Practical Jokes

WE ALL NEED A release from time to time, and occasionally we have the right crew and circumstances to let loose. Your cabin crew is capable of some really devilish pranks.

We have the more mild ones like sticking "CREW USE ONLY" on the bottom of a cute fellow flight attendant. Putting coffee grounds on top of a F/A's suitcase, so when they get it down at the end of a flight, it douses them. Placing whipped butter on the receiver of the galley phone, then calling from one cabin up (when the victim answers the phone, the butter coats far up into the ear). I knew this one male F/A who used to always pass gas in the cockpit. He'd chuckle about it for hours afterwards.

There is nothing like the satisfaction of a successful, well-planned prank. For example, I placed a small cup of dry lemonade powder above my fellow joker friend's jumpseat. When the plane landed and the brakes pulled the airplane's momentum forward, the cup tipped over, and doused his thick black hair with this golden powder. He laughed for a second when he realized what had happened, then headed straight for the nearest toilet – where, incidentally, a large cup of water was propped carefully on top of the door and waiting for him. It drenched him as he entered. Thus the powder hardened along with his hair. The whole crew was in on it. We couldn't stop laughing for the entire deplaning of passengers. What made it more hysterical was that he had a previously scheduled meeting with his supervisor after the flight.

Then there are the jokes we play on the passengers like changing the combination on an abusive traveler's suitcase. Or look frightened every time you pass the "obnoxious but afraid to fly" passengers. A classic one is sending an unknowing F/A to deliver a razor to a man who has a foot-long beard, or a lady with hairy armpits. My favorite was to give out the First Class carnations to the passengers whom we least liked, because we knew that they would always be sent to agricultural inspection when going through Customs in the U.S.A. It never failed in certain airports. Vengeance would be ours, and we would appear generous.

I heard about a cockpit crew playing a joke on a brand new flight attendant. They told her that there was a problem with the landing gear. She was instructed to go out to the middle section of the cabin and jump up and down a couple of times in hopes of dislodging it. It was truly hilarious, but one of the pilots eventually got suspended for it.

Some other jokes include: rolling the butterballs in coffee grounds and serving them to the cockpit as chocolate truffles, making instant dribble glasses by piercing holes in the plastic glasses, shaking up cans of something carbonated and then giving it to a F/A to serve. Icing down the coffee so that when the passenger says that the coffee is ice cold, you know that this time they weren't exaggerating.

When the safety demonstration is not on video, many jokes can be played such as writing something funny on the inside of the safety card like "How do you like my boob job?" Rarely does the F/A look inside before opening and showing the passengers. Or inserting a live air cartridge in the demo life vest – when they pull down in the demonstration, they get a shock and a whole lot of air. I can remember a young F/A actually wetting her pants on that one.

Yes, you might call it juvenile or even silly, but it passes the time and it makes for a much-needed laugh. I can't see the harm in it all as long as it doesn't infringe on personal safety. Laughter is one of the most precious things in this world, and life should not be taken so seriously. Obviously, it is much better to give than it is to receive, but I can tell you honestly, I have received my fair share of abuse as well.

Flight Attitude

ALL THIS RAGGING ON the passengers; what about the mean and nasty flight attendants? Yes, they are out there, too. You're really thirsty and you ask the attendant for two drinks; all they do is sigh, roll their eyes, and hand you your second gluttonous drink.

Your meal is cold and they reply, "What do you expect me to do about it?" They talk about you in the galley, laugh at your faults, and feel abused with every request. They forget everything you ask them for (probably on purpose) and are only happy when you leave. They hide in the back and are never seen again after the service. They ignore the call bells and have tunnel vision as they walk through the aisles ignoring you.

There are also a lot of whiney F/As as well. They could be staying at a $300 a night beautiful hotel in downtown Stockholm, but if there wasn't any hot water for an hour, it was a miserable trip. They would continue to complain about it the whole trip back. I would interject with, "Yeah, but wasn't the city skyline beautiful?" They'd give me a "die leper boy" glare, and go back to their whining.

You can always distinguish a newly hired F/A from one who is bored with it. Maybe it's the look of excitement about the job at hand. Maybe it's the fact that she's flying five or more miles above the ground. Possibly, her excitement could be from never having been to Stockholm before and she has three days in a lovely hotel to discover this new city. All these factors, and more, are compiled in her excited grin. Then she is reminded by the nasty F/A in her crew, "The last time I was there they didn't have any hot water for a whole hour, and it rained the whole time."

I think it's the balance of nature in a way. F/As take more than their share of crap and, to counteract it, release it in different ways.

There are many personalities in the world, and sometimes passengers and F/As are not always going to connect in a harmonious manner. There is no excuse for a rude F/A. Everyone has hard days, but we are trained to fake kindness even when we have feelings of absolute hatred. So if you do encounter an overly rude F/A, get his or her name and write a complaint letter. It will go in their record, and it is more than likely that they have been reported before. They do read your letters, good and bad, and your letters do make a difference. It's really the only effective method of complaining. Anything else is just wasted air.

I once got on a flight and was so badly treated that I swore that I would never fly on that specific airline again. Then I realized I had to; I worked for them.

To Be Or Not To Be?

I SMILED, BENT OVER, and placed the used meal tray on the bottom rung as I had been previously taught by the many F/As before me. All of a sudden and out of nowhere, I felt a heat wave initially strike my head and drench my body. I had heard of similar episodes happening to stroke victims all the time. Was this it? Was it my time? I was only 22 and in fairly good shape. This wasn't right. Was the plane crashing?

An awful stench penetrated my nostrils and made me feel sick, until I realized that someone already had been sick...all over me. I rose in horror. People looked at me, some in terror, others in laughter. Particles dripped off me in a strategic manner. My mind froze, and my body shut down. My whole being was in disbelief. Not even a look of sorrow was spared from the sender.

I ran to the toilet in hopes of a shower or at least a paper towel bath. I was going to be cleaning for quite a while. Very close to quitting, I needed a long think before doing anything rash. I found myself in the toilet, again, contemplating life. For some reason, I seemed to do all my best thinking there.

There are many pros and cons about being a flight attendant. Obviously, there were enough pros to keep the hundreds of thousands, and me, in this job as a career, rather than a hobby.

I started with the good aspects. The perks associated with this job are numerous. We receive service charge (almost free) flights all over the world for our parents and ourselves. Airline employees get discounts on almost everything. We get more than half the month off work. We choose when we work, if at all, and we can change our schedule to suit our lifestyle. We get paid fairly well, considering the amount of time actually on duty. It still is a somewhat glamorous lifestyle. We stay in exciting cities in top-rated hotels all over the world. A trip or two a week breaks up the monotony in life. If you can get over the fact that there are a lot of demanding bastards out there, there are also a lot of interesting people, as well. We meet many different people each trip. I work with many beautiful and fun women. Having lots of time off, I can have two jobs or spend more time with my family. I work for a prosperous airline, and I have a tough union. I'm quite happy with my life and present position.

As I continued to dab at the vomit on my uniform, I was abruptly reminded of the cons. The F/A job is tougher than you think. We are the direct link you have with the company; anything you don't like or can't stand about the airline you tell us, the people who can do absolutely nothing about it. Along with food and drink server, come the jobs of safety professional, nursemaid, babysitter, psychiatrist, in-flight police, seat arranger, problem solver, first aid nurse, counselor, travel agent, cook, social worker, paramedic, janitor, and in-flight mechanic, among other things. While it's a glamorous lifestyle, it's not a glamorous job. For example, you may be on your way to Rio de Janeiro, but you're on your hands and knees cleaning up after someone who has just projectile-vomited in the kitchen and on your jumpseat.

Flights are basically free, but you don't get a seat unless there is an empty seat available. Reserve is torture, because you are never sure when you're going to work next. There is little or no chance of promotion. Pay raises cease after a certain number of years. It's not a respected job, like it once was. Most of my friends are lawyers and doctors, making twice my salary.

When I say I work for the airline, everyone asks, "How long have you been a pilot?" If I decide to answer honestly, they automatically think that I'm gay. When I proposed to my girlfriend (now wife), I got the thumbs-down vote by every member of her family solely based on my job. Her father told me that we wouldn't have his blessing until I got a proper man's job. (They got over it after a while.)

It's not a healthy job with the polar radiation, irregular sleeping patterns and hours, dehydrating altitudes, and always dining out. Our insurance premiums are higher because we are in a higher risk occupation. We have to take your insults and rude comments, while most of the time we would love to give you a piece of our mind. I thank people for their trash. Unfortunately, I answer to all of the following: "hey, you," "steward," "psst!," clearing of the throat, snapping of the fingers, tugging on my uniform, or tapping on my person (although I try to ignore the last two, and deliver a scowl). When I am not flying, I still answer to "excuse me."

I'm the first to clear the dishes and pour the wine at home. The retirement packages for most airlines are bad or nonexistent, and someone has just vomited all over me.

You take the good with the bad. Some quit, but most stay. After a while it's almost an addiction. Most find that after they quit, they are lost without the accustomed get-up-and-go-anywhere-in-the-world lifestyle.

I fly with former accountants, teachers, lawyers, stockbrokers, dentists, nurses, bartenders, financial consultants, chefs, fashion designers, etc., all in search of adventure and something new; some find it and some don't.

Such is life.

Michael

MICHAEL WAS ABOUT 38 years old. He stood 5 foot 10 inches tall. A moustache adorned his smile, and his errant sandy brown hair was graying around the sides. He was one of those people whom everyone liked, and I was no exception. He had been a F/A for about 16 years and absolutely loved his job, and revered all people.

After about three years, my own love of the job had waned, and I was going through the weary notion of calling it quits. No matter what you are or what you are paid, there are always those times when you face your dream and hear some sour notes. This was one of those times for me. People were demanding. I was starting to see a side to human nature that was causing me to be cynical and disgusted. The adventure of new lands was not enough to compensate for what I believed, at the time, to be a drain on my dignity.

I met Michael at a time of inward sighing. After all those years, Michael was still radiantly beaming and sweet. Time after time, he would go out into the aisles and ask passengers if they wanted anything else. That may not sound unheard of to a passenger, but as a F/A, the norm is to wait until asked. I teased him constantly, but secretly I admired him for it.

Michael had a wonderful sense of humor, but never talked badly about anyone. Even the most obnoxious of passengers could not rile him. I had to force a bad comment out of him occasionally, just to make him human, but even then it was a mild one. He was my model of kindness and health; a person whom I wanted to be more like, a figure I respected with all of my heart. Whenever he was in town, my (then) girlfriend and I would take him out to dinner and to the movies. He never spoke of personal relationships, so I didn't know where he stood as far as his private life was concerned. I later found out that he was, indeed, gay, but it didn't matter in the slightest.

It was no surprise that he won an award for F/A of the year. I would tease him about it, but secretly I was envious. He deserved it, and I couldn't believe that the right person was nominated this time. Michael told me that he was very proud of the award. It meant that his father, who had not been very proud of some of the decisions his son had made, would get a First Class ticket to an award banquet in New York.

I saw him last on an extremely hot day in June. He was on his way to a Paris flight, and I was on my way to a Munich flight. I invited him to a barbecue on July 4th, but he told me that he had other plans. I shook his hand and told him that I wished I flew with him more often. He kindly smiled, and we went to our separate flights.

The summer ended and I found myself at home trying to quell the summer's heat. Bored and grumpy, I began to read the company newspaper (one has to be pretty desperate to read that). I got to the obituaries and subconsciously skimmed the names. In small typed letters was Michael's name, base, and the date that he died – a mere ten days after I had spoken to him.

My heart felt as if it was being gripped by daggers. My eyes, already hot, scalded with tears of disbelief. I called a mutual friend, who confirmed that it was our Michael who had passed. He apparently had had the HIV virus for quite some time. Michael had entered the hospital on a Friday with a headache, and died on Saturday afternoon. He was spared the suffering that is traditionally associated with this disease.

The person who made the deepest impression on me in his job and life was gone. I cried for two days straight. To me, it was nothing short of admirable and incredible that he knew of his affliction and yet remained a kind and positive person until the end.

This occupation has an abnormally high rate of homosexual workers, and unfortunately AIDS has claimed many lives in this field. My three roommates in initial training are gone now as well, and I have continued to lose many friends and colleagues through the years. We are all different in this life and choose our various roads accordingly, although in this job the common bond we all seem to share is that we started with adventure in our eyes and passion in our hearts.

Michael's essence remains with me today; it is one of innocence of the heart, goodness in its most raw form. When I remember Michael, my heart seems to beat just a little extra. I saw beyond his preferences into what his soul was. I guess there is a part of me to this day that will never quite understand how a human could be so pure.

8

Life and Death In-Flight

Hold the Mayo

IT WAS A SWELTERINGLY hot August day in Paris. It was the day after Bastille Day (French Independence Day), and we had to work a full flight back to Los Angeles with hangovers. The whole crew had joined in the previous night's celebration, and nobody held back from the free-pouring wine. Of course, the air conditioner in the airplane wasn't working yet, so everyone was sticky and quite aromatic upon boarding.

As a treat, airport catering brought on a crate of Independence Day snacks for the crew and passengers. It was full of incredibly delicious prawn sandwiches. We were starving because our hangovers were wearing off, and hunger was setting in. We ate as much as we could handle, and then passed what was left out to the passengers.

We finally took off and the air conditioning kicked in. The snacks had seemed to cure the hangovers. The blurred details of the previous night were the topic of conversation, and the flight improved with time. We teased one of the F/As (Tammy), because she had been so drunk at the festivities that she had joined a couple of locals in a total striptease. It was very bizarre to witness, because she was one of the shyest girls I had ever flown with prior to this flight. She wouldn't forget that night for a while, no matter how hard she tried.

Two hours into the flight, we were halfway through our meal service when I saw Tammy holding her stomach, grimacing with pain. I was on the meal cart in the other aisle. She continued to work, when all of a sudden she dropped a tray. She quickly left her cart and ran down the aisle for the nearest toilet. I watched with concern and horror as she made it only as far as the last row. She didn't throw up in front of the last row, she threw up all over the last row and all of its occupants.

I quickly helped to clean things up, trying to appease the passengers, but how do you appease someone who has just been sprayed with projectile vomit? We put Tammy in the crew rest area and tried to resume the service. Fifteen minutes later the F/A who replaced her started to go pale – slowly more and more people started to become sick. It was like an epidemic.

I called the cockpit to inform the captain of the dangerous situation that was arising. One of the pilots up front had also taken ill. Something was wrong – hangovers weren't contagious. It had to come from something, but the only thing that we'd eaten or served was...**the sandwiches!!!!!**

The captain declared an in-flight emergency and told us that the nearest landing point would be New York in approximately 90 minutes. I got off the phone with the captain and went to brief the crew, but most of them were in the toilets, sick. There were long lines for every restroom, and we were running out of sick bags. The only F/As still around were Sarah, who was a vegetarian and had not eaten the sandwiches, and myself, but I was fading fast.

I made an announcement informing the passengers of our deviation plans for New York, and the probability of the snacks being the culprit. I also suggested that those passengers who were not sick should pass their sick bag to their nearest neighbor who was ill. When we ran out, I recommended using their pillowcases. Everybody kept handing me their dripping used parcels, but I couldn't take them, because I had nowhere to put them all. I was going to bring a large trash bag around to collect them but by that time I had become sick and ended up throwing up into that bag. It was one big vomit orgy.

We finally landed in New York, greeted by at least 50 ambulances and paramedics. We were all rushed to various hospitals along with the only uneaten prawn sandwich (I was saving it for later) for analysis. The culprit turned out to be the mayonnaise, not the shrimp, as we had suspected.

There was a detailed investigation, afterwards, into the incident. They discovered that the sandwiches had been prepared for a flight that should have left the day before, but had been canceled. They were not intended for our flight. OOPS!

The heat had 48 hours to spoil the mayonnaise and shrimp. No lawsuits ever saw the light of day due to the uncertainty of blame, plus the fact that the airline was already in bankruptcy protection.

It's a humorous memory now that I can look back on it without gagging, but to this day I cannot eat any form of shrimp-based foods, and I am sure that the one statement everyone aboard that flight has in common when ordering a sandwich is:

"Hold the Mayo...Please."

Jet Lag

IF YOU TRAVEL ENOUGH, sooner or later you will fall victim to the ever-popular traveling syndrome we in the flight industry call "hypoboeingtinitus" or "the funk," and more commonly known as jet lag. It is the feeling of severe lack of energy, weird sleeping patterns, always tired, no vigor, depression, and about a day or two of being in a daze.

Some say it's caused by dehydration from the airplane trip, change of time zones, altitude sickness, lack of sleep, and some even attribute it to polar radiation. While all of these may be true, the one factor that I have narrowed it down to is the definite change in sleeping patterns. You arrive in Italy and it may be 3 o'clock in the afternoon, but your body is not convinced and insists that it is midnight.

Other factors include worrying about and anticipation of the trip. Realize that while traveling may be a wondrous occasion, it is quite a stressful one as well. Some prepare too much for their trip, while others not enough. Some people drink too much on the flight (I am more inclined to say that is a hangover instead of jet lag). All of these are contributing factors to this syndrome.

It is a bit odd that the most severe jet lag always occurs on the returning leg of your trip. Then again that could be the result of realizing just how much you spent, or how much weight you've gained. Most probably it was that over-indulgence on your last night there.

A commonly asked question is whether or not we (F/As) get jet lag. The answer is not as easy as a yes or no. Some do and some don't. You'll find that the ones that don't are the ones that fly only international trips.

Speaking for myself, most of the time I don't get jet lag. It's all in the sleep pattern. I can stay awake for 36 hours straight and I can sleep for 20-plus at a time. It is only when I don't disrupt my sleeping pattern that my jet lag sets in. For example, if I have two weeks off and I don't fly anywhere, my sleep pattern returns to that of a normal person – sleeping and waking at roughly the same times, day in and day out. This seems to disturb my pattern of disrupted sleep. I know it is fairly hard to comprehend, but it isn't if you live it.

Here is a list of some preventative jet lag measures. While many of these tips seem like common sense, a lot of the time we seem to check that in along with our luggage.

Frank's Ten Top Tips to Prevent or Minimize Jet Lag

1. Try to get some sleep on the plane. You'd be surprised how many people force themselves to stay awake for the movie.

2. Don't overdo it on the booze or sleeping pills, on the flight or at your final destination.

3. Drink lots of water. Try to hydrate (water) yourself more than the flight dehydrates you.

4. Take supplemental vitamins before, during, and after your trip, and moisturizer is a good item to have nearby at all times.

5. When you arrive, try to adapt to the new time of day immediately. For example, force yourself to stay awake until the time of day you would normally go to sleep back home.

6. Go for a long walk or a run when you settle in. The more oxygen, fresh air, and exercise, the better.

7. Don't try to see every sight in one day. That is, of course, as long as you have more than one day.

8. If you are returning from holiday or a long business trip, allow a couple of days after to recover. Don't go into work the next day.

9. Eat lots of vegetables and healthy foods, or at least bring some supplemental bran with you.

10. Don't worry so much. Try to have fun – even if you are on business or the trip is costing you a fortune. Life is an adventure, and this is just another chapter of it.

While I'm at it I am going to give you a few "keep well in-flight" suggestions as well.

1. Wear shoes or at least keep your socks on at all times (especially in the lavatories).

2. If you are sick (I mean sick, not the sniffles), don't fly. Traveling while ill is not a healthy idea for you or the passengers around you. If you have a medical condition, you probably should get your physician's okay to travel.

3. Know where your sick bag is, and use it when necessary. It's much more absorbent than your partner's shoulder or the flight attendant's back.

4. Bring Dramamine if you are prone to seasickness; Tylenol PM works great, too.

5. Bring some anti-acid tablets (i.e., Rolaids, Tums, etc.) because airline food doesn't settle well with some people.

6. Don't put any important medication in your checked luggage; put it in your carry-on bag.

7. If you can only drink mineral water as opposed to tap water, bring your own. When we run out of bottled water, we refill bottles from the tap.

8. If you have a stinky foot condition, foot powder or Odor Eaters will aid in better neighborly relations.

9. If mental health or high blood pressure is a potential problem, earplugs will prevent the murder of the little brat who keeps yelling and crying.

10. Even if it is the hottest summer in ages, bring a sweater or a coat. The airplane almost always ends up being on the chilly side and the destination's weather is usually uncertain.

Here's to your good travel health, and may your jet lag be minimal.

Out With It

I WAS ALWAYS THE joker. The one who would jump at any chance to make other people laugh, and everyone knew it. I had just finished a birthday layover in San Francisco. The crew and I were waiting for the plane to be serviced before we could board and work home. To have a little privacy before the flight, the crew gathered in a corner of the airport away from the passengers. I had a mild hangover but a happy memory. A bite of pizza, a quick thought to call my mother, followed by a muffled thump, occurred in the matter of a half second. It took a couple of seconds before I fully realized that my airway was completely blocked.

Panic set in quickly. I immediately looked around for a chair to give myself a couple of self-Heimlich thrusts. It never occurred to me to turn to my crew and seek help (especially odd because my wife was one of the crew members). Instead, I nervously walked around with a piece of cheese hanging from the side of my mouth and searched for something. Every seat had a person and, although I tried not to make a scene, people looked at me awkwardly. Every second seemed like an eternity and I was scared.

I turned to the crew with a bright red face, a stagger, and a convulsive wince. Hoping for a reaction, I got the wrong one; they laughed. To them, I was doing another one of my skits. My wife looked at me and, as I started to turn blue, I screamed help with my eyes. I surrendered to her and accepted that I was leaving this world 25 years to the day that I entered.

"Roger, he's choking! Give him the Heimlich maneuver!" My wife screamed at the nearest male crew member.

Roger, a somewhat effeminate middle-aged man, jumped to his feet and ran to me, waving his hands in the air. He grabbed me, spun me around, and performed the maneuver on me. It wasn't a powerful thrust but just enough to dislodge the piece of pizza. I spat it out and collapsed to my knees. I was drenched in sweat but the color started to come back to my face. The color went from blue to red, then to normal, only to return to red with embarrassment.

I tried to play it off with remarks like, "The pizza here is a killer," or "I was choking, not joking."

The hundred staring passengers in the boarding area weren't exactly sure if it was all real or a hoax. It was probably the most embarrassing moment of my life, but from a hindsight point of view I am glad it happened. It made me understand a few things more clearly. We once had a passenger who, after lodging a piece of candy in his throat, ran to the lavatory. We found him dead an hour later. I never could understand why he ran from the very people who could help him. Now I do because it was what I had initially done. Causing a scene or admitting weakness is a terrifying prospect, and all rationality disappears.

If you are choking on the airplane, your flight attendants are trained to help. If you can't make a noise, make yourself noticed, cross your arms, and clench your neck. We will know what to do from there. Cause a scene! It's better to be embarrassed than deceased.

On the flight over, Roger and I had previously teased one another about my straight macho ways and his limp wrists and feminine mannerisms. It was all in good fun but, Roger, although I have said it many times before, thank you for your saving grace and may God bless those life-saving wrists. I owe you a lot more than you could ever imagine.

Sterile Cockpit

ONE DAY MY WIFE (who is also a flight attendant) approached me with a quiz that she got out of a women's magazine. She laughed when I expressed concern about it being a fertility quiz. She wasn't trying to hint at something but was just curious about our status. After a small amount of opposition, I agreed to take part.

There was a separate section for men, and it was based on total honesty. It gave you a statement and if you strongly agreed you got 3 points; moderate agreement, 2 points; disagreement, 1 point; and strong disagreement, 0 points. I made myself cozy on the other side of the room and began my task.

1. I rarely fly more than once a month. Answer: Obviously 0 points.

2. I have a normal sleeping pattern and rarely disrupt it. Answer: 0 points; woo hoo, 2 for 2.

3. I seldom encounter electromagnetic screening security systems like the ones found in airports? Answer: 0 points. Can you see where this is going?

4. I always eat a well balanced diet with basically the same daily eating times. Answer? You got it, 0 points.

This was getting a bit ridiculous; I had to get a point sooner or later.

5. Computer screens are not a part of your daily routine. Answer: 0 points.

6. I have never had a sexually transmitted disease. Answer: 3 points. There we go, I was on a roll.

7. Alcohol consumption doesn't take place more than 2 times a week. Answer: 0 points. Oh man, that wasn't fair.

8. Travel is not a major part of my job. Answer: 0 points. This had to be some kind of joke.

It went on with similar statements. I am sure you get the idea. Well my grand total out of a possible 30 points was three measly points. I was afraid to turn the page for my result.

I read the top results first as it went on about super sperm and strong probabilities of children and so forth. When I got to my result it said in a nutshell that "In the curious event that my sperm were still alive, hopefully there are wheelchairs down there to get them to the egg meeting in time. Look at the bright side, it just means that it will probably take more meetings, wink wink."

Well, that was fun. My wife got five out of 30, beating me because of some menstrual cycle question. We laughed it off, thankful that we weren't trying at the time.

Several trips later it was becoming very clear to me that an unusual amount of my airline friends and co-workers were having problems conceiving. Out of ten (couple) friends, two had children, one didn't want children, two were waiting (of which we were one), and five were having problems. Two of those five were currently undergoing fertility treatment and IVF (In Vitro Fertilization). If my math is correct, that is a remarkable 50% who were having conception difficulties with a high-end possibility of an amazing 80%. Now on every trip I hear of some crew member going through some kind of fertility treatment. I know that in the real world that 15% can expect to experience difficulties conceiving, but in the airline world it seems to be quite a bit higher.

It got me thinking about my own fertility and the quiz that I had previously laughed off. So on a layover in some remote city, I secretly went off and spent $180 to masturbate into a cup (because, of course, such tests aren't covered by our company's insurance policy).

I called up a week later to find out my results. They said that my motility was found to be poor. Which meant, you got it, "my fishies were poor swimmers, and would probably have trouble getting to the egg meeting on time." He went on to say, " Look on the bright side...." You know the rest.

So, to all of my flying colleagues and frequent flyers out there having similar difficulties, this is just to tell you that you are not alone.

In a Puff of Smoke

WE ARE COMING TO a point in the flying industry that smoking may never be allowed again. Smokers are suing the tobacco industry; flight attendants are suing the airlines for secondhand smoke inhalation which has resulted in cancer. The government is beginning to outlaw smoking everywhere, including airplanes. Airlines are succumbing to the pressure, and the smoker is starting to accept it as fact. Speaking for the majority of the F/A population worldwide, I have to say, THANK GOD!

There are no more massive seating mix-ups as far as non-smoking and smoking sections go. Smoke clouds aren't hovering over the seats. There is less danger of fires. You and I don't get off the plane smelling like cigarette butts. The air is much healthier, and the atmosphere is quite a bit happier.

The old policy of "non-smoking sections" was moronic at best. You could be seated in row 35 (a non-smoking row), only to have the smoking section start at row 36. Technically, you were in the non-smoking section, although you were inhaling smoke rings through your nostrils the entire flight.

The passenger who smokes a pack or more a day, who can't handle a long flight without lighting up, has several options:

1. Nicotine (tastes horrible, but works) gum.
2. Nicotine patches.
3. Chewing tobacco (please don't hand us your spit cup).
4. Freak out, and yearn for the next cigarette.
5. Sneak a cigarette in one of the restrooms, and get arrested upon landing.
6. Stay home!

I would say that #2 would be your best choice, but, then again, I went into the cockpit one day and saw the captain smoking. I told him about the patches, and he rolled up his sleeves and remarked, "You mean these?" He exposed two of them on his arm. (I thought that was supposed to be dangerous.)

I used to be a smoker, but it's frightening to see the withdrawal that some go through. I have seen a woman in tears, a man bring his own hypnotist, and another have a complete anxiety attack. He ended up hitting a F/A. If you can't last ten hours without a cigarette, you should seek professional help.

The safety aspect is a valid point as well. A test was done on the oxygen masks of an older 747 and found that only 60% of the masks dropped in the smoking section, and 99% dropped in the non-smoking section. The nicotine and tar had sealed shut the compartments containing the masks. That would make for a depressing decompression.

There were also people who left lit cigarettes in their ashtrays, which would fall onto the ground, or their seats, and start fires. Many incidents have been caused that way. You might come back with the argument, "Isn't it more dangerous risking someone sneaking a cigarette in the restroom?" No, not really. There are automatic extinguishers in the trash bins. If you do decide to sneak one in there, realize there are smoke detectors in there. Yes, I know that there are ways around that, but the smell will tell on you. When you are caught, you will be met by authorities and fined a minimum of $2,000. All the F/A needs is a witness, who is probably standing outside the lav door waiting to use it.

Now even airports are going non-smoking, except for the little glass rooms with seats and overflowing ashtrays. It's called the Smoking Room, but we call it the aquarium. The smoky air looks like murky water, and everyone inside has their lips puckered like fish. You can smoke in there, but you end up smelling 50 times worse and, I am sorry to say it, you look...well, stupid. Everyone who looks in sees all of you crowded around an ashtray looking like animals at feeding time. It's like a free cancer exhibition at the airport. But it will solve your current need, and you won't offend anyone's right to clean air.

The Ivy League

I WAS SO EXCITED to be at my new base, and ready to experience traveling to the other half of the world. I was setting out on a six-day trip laying over in Paris, Frankfurt, and Hamburg. A bit nervous about being slotted in as the purser of the flight, I wanted to make a good impression on my new flying colleagues. All went as planned until two minutes after take-off, when the leg that I had been unconsciously scratching started to burn badly. I went to the lavatory to investigate and was mildly concerned when a light rash started to appear. Not thinking too much about it, I went back to work.

Hours later when the service ended I sat down to have a quick bite, my leg started to throb. Ooh, how one scratch filled me with delightful relief. Excusing myself to the lavatory once again, I found that the light rash had spread and now was looking like strawberry jam. I looked at myself in the mirror and searched for an answer. A light bulb went off in my mind. I thought back to the recent weekend camping trip, when my girlfriend and I had discovered nature. We had slipped off the beaten path and engaged in a romantic roll in the hay, which must have been...**poison ivy**! I come from the West Coast where I was familiar with poison oak, but knew nothing about the conditions or ramifications of the dreaded ivy. In the mirror I saw my facial expression turn from concentration to fear.

I didn't have a friend or crew member to turn to. I tried the 70-year-old lady working the First Class galley because of her grandmotherly like appearance.

"Uh, say, Edith, what do you know about poison ivy?"

"Oh, that is a nasty plant and should be avoided at all costs. I remember my husband catching a dose of that in 1963, or was it 1964? No, it was definitely 1963, because JFK was running for office...Hang on, it was 1962. That was some year, I remember going to the store and...."

"Uh, thanks, Edith, would you excuse me? I have to go to the back for a second."

I was starting to suffer, and every time I went to the restroom it seemed to be getting worse, spreading over a wider terrain on my body. Unfortunately, the rash had included the area that I feared most...the privates.

On the bus ride into Paris, the entire lower half of my body yearned for just a mere scratch or a slight rub up against anything. I was fairly subdued to the rest of the crew. I thanked them but politely turned down any dinner or sightseeing invitations for the layover. I got to my room and trembled as I ripped off my uniform as if it was on fire. There I stood in shock: naked, with one foot on the bidet and the other on the toilet, staring at the bathroom mirror in horror at the rash attacking my body.

I went out to the local pharmacy, but of course in Europe they don't have poison ivy – or anything similar, for that matter. When I was finally able to explain in broken English and a bad French accent, the elderly lady handed me a tube of medicine designed for insect bites. I didn't have a clue on my next plan of action. When a curious tune that I was humming in the back of my mind became more clear, I started to sing.

"POISON IIIIIIIVY, POISON IIIIIIIIIIIVY, When the something comes a sleeping the something something comes a creeping all around. There may be a potion, some calamine lotion!"

"CALAMINE LOTION! Ah voules vous calamine lotion?"

Luckily, she didn't throw me out for being a nutter. She handed me a bottle of Calidryl, which was their version of calamine lotion. I asked for four more bottles, found the nearest grocery store, grabbed two loaves of bread and two bottles of cheap red wine, and barricaded myself in my room. There I lay for 24 hours hardened from waist to toe in crusty calamine lotion, watching nonstop CNN, swigging red wine, and humming that stupid ivy song.

My girlfriend called me up in my delirium and started the conversation with, "Uh, honey, what do you know about poison ivy?" All I could do was laugh and cry at the same time.

The Booze Cruise

WE ALL KNOW THAT flying is usually a sign of vacation, adventure, reunion, or big business deals, and most people could use a drink or two. I know I can, when I'm on a flight. Well, here is a very important piece of advice: **Know when to stop!**

If you have a control problem on the ground, don't start on an airplane. Now that all alcohol on most international flights is complimentary, I've seen more vacations ruined, business meetings blown, and more holidays wrecked by alcohol.

What people don't realize is that your tolerance at 30,000 feet shrinks by 30%. So, if your tolerance is normally six cocktails, your limit should be four. You may drink four and say, "I feel all right." Wait until you land. There are several theories about this situation. The scientific theory is that, at that altitude, the cabin pressure is such that the alcohol concentrates in your bloodstream and sends a more powerful dose to your brain.

The general theory is that the altitude dehydrates you, and the alcohol dehydrates you ten times more. Dehydration is also the cause for most cases of jet lag.

My theory is that most people get bored and lose track of how many drinks they have had. Alcohol makes you forget that boredom. Once the feeling starts wearing off, you need more drinks to continue forgetting how bored you are (got that?). All three theories are probably fairly accurate in their own right.

I've not only experienced extreme intoxication firsthand, but I've witnessed the worst. I've seen sophistication turn into infancy; guys vomit on their girlfriends, and vice versa; passports, tickets, and bags get lost; arrests made at airports; husbands cheat on their wives, wives catch them; fist fights break out; children left behind, taken away, vomited on, etc. I had a man on board who had saved all of his life to take his wife on an around-the-world vacation. He overdid the celebrating and ended up in a New York jail for the first ten days of his trip. I even had a man try to open the airplane door at 30,000 feet. Need I go on?

PEOPLE! Just because it's free, it doesn't mean you have to pour as much down your throat as you can in the allotted time. If you don't drink Scotch at home, don't start on the flight. It's strange how some people forget all the rules of drink when they take a flight. I have to admit my own guilt as well.

The old silly saying still holds true:

> Beer to wine; feeling fine,
> Liquor to beer; never fear.
> But beer or wine to liquor;
> never sicker.

And most importantly, know when to say "when"!

It may sound preposterous, but I can't tell you how many people I've seen start off with two champagnes for pre-departure, have a couple of gin and tonics for the beverage service, followed by four or five glasses of wine with their meal, a glass of port or two with their cheese, and to top it off a couple of cognacs for dessert. Now, if you were counting, that was 11 to 12 drinks times 30%. That's the equivalent of 15 drinks, and you have managed to mix just about every alcohol group that exists. An instant recipe for one of the worst hangovers ever.

If you don't feel bad after that, then you are too far gone to save. For those of you who haven't experienced it: you have been warned.

The End of the Journey

I HAD SEEM THEM before; the lines in their faces were vaguely familiar. They were an elderly couple I had served on the way to Europe. Since I see thousands of faces a month, remembering this couple pleased me. What stood out about them was their love for one another, and their longevity. In a world where divorce is much too common, it was wonderful to see such a successful marriage in progress. The fact that they had never been out of the United States in their 70-odd years was also somewhat amazing to me.

"Hello again. How was your trip?" I asked, as they were stowing their bags.

"Oh, hello," she replied somewhat startled, but recognized me after a moment.

"We feel somewhat embarrassed that we haven't done this sooner," she blushed.

"The dollar isn't worth very much, that's for sure, but we had a wonderful trip," he said, with a smile shining through his tired exterior. The flight was approximately 11 hours long, and they looked as if a good sleep was in order.

The flight continued on, and everyone anticipated our arrival. We served the final meal about two hours out, and I noticed that the elderly woman was awake, but her husband slumbered on peacefully. She waved her hand delicately as if to say no meal for them. It was a completely full airplane (i.e., noisy), so it was nice to see anyone sleep well. We arrived in San Francisco, and all of the passengers got off. I regretted the fact that I had forgotten to say good-bye to the sweet old couple sitting by the window.

As I got my bags ready, I noticed the couple still there with the lady waving her hand, motioning me her way. I rushed to her side, noticing her husband still fast asleep.

"I'm afraid my husband has passed on," she muttered quietly as the tears traced the creases down her face.

I heard "passed out" so I asked, "What can I do to help? Is he on medication? Has this sort of thing happened before?"

"No, I'm afraid he has been dead for the last five hours," the tears, by now welling up like dams in her eyes.

Realizing what she had said, I reached for the carotid artery on his neck – he was, indeed, dead. We called for an ambulance, and they were taken away. I got to the hotel that night in shock. The feeling of death was fresh in my mind, along with the image of the woman's face, and her tears. She apparently had discovered her husband's fate 30 minutes after it had happened, but said nothing, knowing that there were no empty seats. She wanted to spare him the indignity of being stared at by the curious.

I felt guilty that when I had first met them, I thought how sweet it was that they were seeing Europe before they died. I wondered how much farther his soul had to rise to get to heaven. The thought of the sweet lady sitting next to her dead husband for four and a half hours and saying nothing haunted me. I put my head down, cried, and longed for another day.

9

Being Frank

Airline of Choice

IT IS IMPORTANT TO realize that most of the big airlines are very similar. Whatever one does, the other hears about and tries to copy. If Joe's Airlines serve lemon-scented armpit tissues, then Ed's Airways will eventually follow suit. The main difference is the destinations and the frequencies of flights. Not to say you're going to like them all equally, because you're going to have positive experiences on some, more than on others, and that's going to be your airline of choice. Just realize that there are good and bad flights with every carrier, along with good and bad crews.

It's all just the luck of the draw. One passenger will vow never to fly with my airline again, while on the very same flight someone else will declare it his or her new favorite carrier. Generally speaking, a more enjoyable flight is one that isn't full. As a fellow F/A puts it, "Every empty seat has a smile, but all of the others have an ass in it... literally."

Empty flights are the best, but if it's a normal occurrence on a certain carrier, then it will certainly result in cutbacks and turn out to be not so special . . . fast.

This one has prettier servers, or that one has better meals, etc. What it boils down to is which airline goes where, when, and costs the least. You may say never again, but if the price is right, you'll be back.

If you're on business and your company is paying, then it's a matter of which airline has a better frequent flier mileage scheme, and which one you have more of a chance of getting an upgrade.

It's only when the factors are the same that the small perks (airline lounges, service features, special luggage check-in, friendlier staff, etc.) make a difference in choice. I think safety and fleet age (average age of the airplanes) should be a main concern, but are factors normally overlooked. When it comes to the flight attendants, we are all just the polyester-dressed workers that try to make do with what our airline supplies us with.

The following is a favorite short story on airlines:

A gorgeous flight attendant was in her uniform for a flight back to her base. It was an irregular operation, so she was flying back on a different airline. The seat next to her was free, so an admiring man from nearby was keen to snatch up the opportunity. He smiled broadly as she returned a courteous but disinterested smile. He couldn't make out the uniform she was wearing because it was unlike the working staff's outfit. In an attempt to make polite conversation and to find out whom she worked for, he leaned over and said, "So do you love to fly and it shows?"

She looked over, smiled, and said politely, "No, no, that's not me." She quickly turned away and pretended to read.

"Are you something special in the air?"

This time she rolled her eyes and tried to convey her annoyance. "No, not that one either." No smile or courtesy was shown.

He thought about it for a moment, smiled, and replied, "Do you fly the friendly skies?"

Quite upset at this point, she turned to the man and said, "Will you just f*** off and leave me alone!"

He replied, confidently nodding his head, "Aahaahhhh, Pan Am."

Pan American Airways (PAN AM)

Their motto was "You can't beat the experience." Not many people did in their prime. They once were the greatest airline in the world, regarded as a highly respected operation that carried hundreds of millions worldwide to their destinations and back. Theirs was the third most recognized symbol in the world besides the golden arches of McDonald's, and Coca-Cola.

Sadly, it all came to an end. Due to poor management, bad decisions, deregulation, no domestic routes, the Lockerbie tragedy, the Gulf War, and the selling off of their most lucrative routes, they were forced to close their doors in 1991.

I am proud to say that I once worked for Pan Am. I pray that it will stay in people's memories forever – not of the troubled last few years, but the great airline it used to be. To the hundreds of thousands who worked for them at one time or another, I salute you, and hope you never forget as well.

Canceled

CANCELLATIONS ARE TRULY a pain in the neck, but they are a fact of life in the game of flying. You had trouble getting the time off from work. Driving to the airport was a hassle, with traffic and parking. Just when you think you're in the clear, an announcement is made stating that your flight is experiencing mechanical difficulties.

"Wait a minute," you say. "This is not possible." This factor was not taken into consideration of your overall flight plans. It's not supposed to happen, but unfortunately it does. If you fly once in a while, sooner or later, you will come across it. If you are a frequent flyer, you know the deal all too well.

As I write this section I am afraid to go to the ice machine in my hotel. This time we have canceled, and the airline has put the passengers at the same hotel as the crew. The passengers were all boarded when the cancellation was declared, so they have all seen my face and do not forget easily. All I need is to hear somebody tell me how badly they've been inconvenienced, just one more time! I have been inconvenienced, too. I understand.

The worst thing about this cancellation is that I have to take the same flight out with the same passengers the next day. I overheard a few passengers remark earlier that they felt sorry for us tomorrow. Believe me, so do I!

Nobody enjoys cancellations, but in comparison to the number of flights that go out successfully, as planned, the percentages are small. However, if it happens to you twice in five years, you tend to think, "Oh, this always happens to me."

Statistics show that approximately two out of 100 flights cancel, and only six out of 100 experience mechanical delays – except for the summer of 2000, but I will get to that in a later chapter.

It's very important that you understand one thing as you're screaming at your nearest flight attendant or ground agent: **it is all in the interest of your safety**. If it takes an extra two hours to fix a fuel valve or four hours to mend a hydraulic leak, then accept it as a necessary item. Grab a magazine and a cup of coffee, and try to understand. There is a reason that the plane can't go to your destination just yet, and that reason is that it is not completely safe for travel. It's when they go despite mechanical problems that you have to start wondering about the airline you're flying with.

With all the recent news about airlines and their safety records, safety should be the top priority when choosing a carrier. When you do experience this sort of delay and/or cancellation, remember this: the airline is responsible for payment and expenses due to this inconvenience. They have a contract with you to get you from point A to point B on the specified date and time. If anything goes wrong once you get to point A, then they have not fulfilled their side of the deal and must rectify it. Any hotel bills, misconnecting flights, and meal expenses should be covered. I'm not recommending that you go crazy in costs, because they usually have limits set up, but use it to the maximum.

Some airlines handle it better than others do, while some are laughable. Our flight, for example, was handled quite well. While the wait was occurring, passengers got a ten-dollar voucher for any of the facilities in the airport. When the cancellation notice was made, they were put up at a very nice hotel with dinner, breakfast, a new flight time the next morning, and a free 15-minute long distance phone call.

It may not seem like much, but with 300 people, it adds up. I have heard of stories of what other airlines had to offer, and it wasn't comparable. One airline recently got into trouble because they had passengers waiting for 34 hours at the gate without so much as a meal voucher. You can count on being well handled in these irregularities by a strong and lucrative airline, or you take your chances with the brink-of-bankruptcy budget airlines. Then again you probably pay more for the bigger ones, so it's all a crap-shoot anyway.

Unfortunately, when incurring a mechanical problem, while the announcements may be truthful on the nature of the problem, they are usually not truthful on the estimated length of time it will take to rectify it. So when they say it will be a 15-minute delay, it's more like you'll see 45 minutes; when they say an hour, it's more like two or three. It's when they say it will be about three hours or more, it's more than likely that the flight is on a decision, and it doesn't look good. A decision basically means that the airline is deciding if the flight is going to go at all, and you had better mentally prepare for the worst.

It's not that they like lying to you, but if they told you the truth just imagine the chaos 300 people could cause with their connecting flights, special situations, and general confusion. Plus, if they say three hours and you go wandering off and by a lucky turn of events the problem is fixed or the aircraft is changed, we're ready to go, but you're out purchasing duty-free. So they play it very cautiously, never divulging too much information.

Tomorrow, when I get on that flight, some of you are going to find me somewhat unsympathetic, and when you get on a plane in another similar situation you might find the flight attendants the same way. Realize that we're not uncaring, but there are just so many complaints, insults, and how-inconvenienced-you-are remarks that we can and will take. How would you have felt if we went with the lavatories not able to flush on a 12-hour flight, or an engine that had a warning light on?

When it comes to mechanical aspects, the flight attendants can do nothing to repair them, only report them. When you see them at the ice machine in the hotel, just smile and leave them alone, at least until the next day. They are tired and irritated, too. All airlines go through mechanical problems. Refer to "The Workhorse" chapter to understand more. It doesn't help to scream at the staff; they know that you're inconvenienced. It's nobody's fault. At the end of the day, if you miss a connecting flight or a business meeting, fail to meet up with a loved one, or start the holiday off a little bit late, remember the most important thing: Your safety has not been compromised, and you will live another day.

Some passengers have not been as lucky.

The Golden Rule

IF THERE WERE BUT one aspect that you took away with you from this book, besides the entertainment and tips, I would hope it was my Golden Rule of dining and traveling: "Don't bite the hand that feeds you."

It sounds clear, easy enough, basic common sense, but you would be surprised to see how many neglect that advice.

I have worked as a busboy, waiter, bartender, and now as a flight attendant, and I have seen the things that servers do to get their vengeance on nasty customers. Some of it has scared me into trying to spread this rule to as many people as possible. Now, this is not meant as a threat but merely a warning, or a piece of sound advice. While I am not in favor of such vengeance, I do agree that some of it is justified from time to time; people who serve you are not your punching bag or your tool to yell at to relieve the stress and frustrations of life.

If you have a legitimate reason, that's different. Make sure someone knows of your problem, but there is a difference between complaining diplomatically and making an ass of yourself. If you don't get a satisfactory response, get names and write letters – and if that fails, fly another airline. If you're in a restaurant, leave a bad (or no) tip, and never go there again.

If you insist on being the nastiest passenger or customer possible, I recommend you bring your own food, drink, and maybe your own gas mask. While I will spare you and not get into some of the more horrific offenses that I have unfortunately witnessed throughout the years, I will tell you a story of a flight attendant I used to fly with. I will call her Mary. She was the sweetest and most shy F/A I had ever met. She was almost always in a good mood. She would never speak badly of anyone and would not listen to or spread gossip (which is a favorite pastime for many F/As). One day Mr. Nasty Passenger was livid and yelled at her non-stop all flight. She was very apologetic and kind, but it didn't appease him. Nevertheless, she was not in the least fazed by his behavior. Thinking back on past flights with her, I never saw her allow anyone nasty get to her.

I had a drink with her on the layover. After a few drinks I asked her how she stayed so calm and was able to take all of that abuse. Maybe she'd had a bit too much to drink that night, but she let me in on her little secret. Every night before a flight she would eat a ton of Brussels sprouts. They were her favorite vegetable, but unfortunately and without fail they caused her the worse case of gas the next day. So, when any of the passengers caused her undue grief she would make the air intolerable for them. Nobody would suspect that someone so cute and innocent could possibly make such a horrible smell. When I thought back about it, I did notice a rancid smell coming from that area on that flight.

Mary would just smile and unload. She had it down to an art, but admitted that it was more effective if they were sitting on the aisle. She blushed and continued, "If that didn't work, I would spit in their drink."

You would never have thought it by looking at her. Just imagine what others are capable of, if the sweet ones can do that. This shouldn't spark fear among you, but it should encourage awareness that such activity is out there and common sense precautions should prevail.

The next time you are about to cause a nasty scene with your waiter, bartender, or F/A, remember my Golden Rule, because they could be loaded with Brussels sprouts, or worse!

Air Outrage

RAGE IS DEFINED AS a violent anger; to speak, act, or move with unrestrained emotion.

"Air rage" is that behavior while flying. There is "road rage" in traffic, as I am sure there is "sea rage" on cruise ships and "rail rage" on trains. I have even seen after-Christmas shoppers react in a way that would qualify as "on-sale-rage."

Stress is the main cause of air rage. Traveling is extremely stressful, more for some than others. You had a difficult time finalizing details at home; traffic to the airport was a nightmare; lines were horrendous checking in; and now the flight is delayed four hours, making your connecting flight impossible. Stress has the power to transform a kind elderly woman into a Tyrannosaurus Rex. You're in an unfamiliar place, surrounded by unfamiliar people; you can lash out in ways never experienced before. It's the emotions of anger and fear rolled into one.

I must confess that on occasion I have felt like hitting a couple of the super-obnoxious passengers. What helped me through those times is a little game that my grandfather taught me when I was a child. It's the old adage, "Put yourself in the other person's shoes." I don't have to agree with the person's actions, I merely try to understand the situation. I ask myself, "How would I feel if I was in his shoes? What would I do? How would I react?" Next time you get angry and can't comprehend someone's actions, try it. You might be surprised by what you discover.

There was a case a while back where a gate agent had his neck broken by a passenger. The passenger alleged it was the gate agent who initially attacked him. He claimed he broke the gate agent's neck while trying to defend himself. It's a bit hard to believe, but possible. The passenger was acquitted of all charges. Some would say it was an unfair verdict, but you can't actually know unless you were there. He had a fair trial and justice was supposedly served. They classified it as "air rage," but a more appropriate term would be "airline rage." Were the passenger's language and physical actions abusive? Probably. Was the gate agent rude, and could he have handled the matter in a more professional manner? Again, probably. Did the passenger take into consideration that the gate agent had just been yelled at by 200 passengers from the previously canceled flight? Probably not. Did the gate agent take into account that this man was traveling with a newborn infant and a sick wife? Once again, probably not.

Just about every week you hear on the news of some form of air rage attack: *Rock Star Urinates On Stewardess, Evangelist Assaults Flight Attendant.* There was even a case where a man broke into the cockpit and attacked the pilots. Five passengers had to wrestle him to the ground; unfortunately, they restrained him a bit too hard and the assailant died.

I have witnessed passengers verbally abusing, hitting, spitting on, and throwing items at my fellow co-workers. All of which is considered a form of air rage. There is absolutely no excuse for assault on an aircraft. Assault is illegal in day-to-day life, but in the air it carries a much stiffer penalty.

Are the cases of stress-related air rage a wake-up call for the airlines? Does this send a message that treating passengers like cattle is unacceptable and potentially dangerous? No, because the airlines know that more staff per passenger means a higher ticket price. They also know that when the general public chooses airlines, the main deciding factor is the ticket price, not customer service. It's all a matter of supply and demand. If the demand is constant, the supply will remain constant as well.

The second main cause of air rage is liquor. I was working a flight from Bombay to Frankfurt where a short Italian man enroute to New York was upset because I had cut him off from alcohol privileges. He seemed intoxicated, and I have no problem stepping in and taking precautionary measures with such passengers. He stood his ground as I stood mine. After a lot of yelling on his part, he took a swing at me and missed badly. The other crew members notified the cockpit, and the captain sent his rather bulky first officer to assist me. We informed the man if he didn't sit down and be quiet for the remainder of the flight, he would be arrested in Frankfurt.

"Good, I always wanted a vacation in Germany," he replied, his speech slurred.

He continued to yell and, when he received no satisfaction, took a swing at the first officer and missed again. We tackled him, handcuffed his hands behind his back, and locked him in the lavatory, where he proceeded to pass out until we landed. He was arrested and sentenced to three months in jail. Not exactly the vacation he was hoping for. I guess that could have been called a case of "whiskey rage."

Frankly Speaking

ON THE AIRPLANE, AS in real life, we say one thing and mean another. It is a common tradition, and unfortunately you need to read between the lines. Here is a little insight into the various definitions of the things that a F/A says. First will be the saying, followed by the actual meaning.

For example:

What we say (Wws.) "I recommend the short ribs today."
What we mean (Wwm.) "We're just about out of chicken."

Wws.   "Ground agents will answer all of your connection and other questions when we land."
Wwm.   "We don't have the foggiest notion."

Wws.   "Yes sir, they could hold the plane for the connecting passengers."
Wwm.   "Don't count on it, pal."

Wws.   "We have a delay of about 20 or 30 minutes."
Wwm.   "Count on at least two hours."

Wws.   "In a water landing, please board the nearest available life raft."
Wwm.   "Start praying."

Wws.   "The departure is on a decision."
Wwm.   "We ain't going nowhere!"

Wws.   "This toilet is broken."
Wwm.   "Someone vomited or urinated all over the floor, and there is no way I'm cleaning it up."

Wws.   "I'm sorry you didn't get your meal choice."
Wwm.   "Stop being such a cry baby, and get a life."

Wws.   "There is a bar set up in the back for all drink requests."
Wwm.   "Get up and get it yourself."

Wws.   "I'll be right back."
Wwm.   "If I'm not back in 15 minutes, don't count on it."

Wws.   "Would you care for a seat belt extension?"
Wwm.   "Time for a diet."

Wws.   "You want me to hang up your coat? What seat are you in?"
Wwm.   "You're not from the Economy section are you?"

Wws.   "I'm sorry, we closed the alcohol bar about a half hour ago."
Wwm.   "You're drunk, and we're cutting you off."

Wws.   "Sorry for the inconvenience."
Wwm.   "Give us a break."

Wws.   "The coats go in the overhead compartments."
Wwm.   "There are no closets."

Wws.   "Due to circumstances beyond our control."
Wwm.   "It's not our fault, don't blame us."

Wws.   "We're not allowed to give out our layover hotel information."
Wwm.   "Not interested."

Wws.   "Yes, it's mineral water."
Wwm   "Tap water has minerals in it too."

Wws.   "Sorry, we don't have any newspapers today."
Wwm.   "Papers are only for Business and First Class."

Wws.   "We have a limited selection of magazines today."
Wwm.   "There is only *Mustang Monthly* left."

Wws.   "Your child sure is an active one."
Wwm.   "Do you mind controlling your little brat?"

The Workhorse

THE AIRPLANE IS A marvelous invention. It can fly thousands and thousands of miles on a single journey. What used to take days merely takes hours. Every model has newer technology, from propellers to jet engines, glass cockpits to the new Boeing 777, private video screens and fax modems to satellite link-ups. The airplanes of today are flying higher and faster than ever before. If they're so advanced, why do they seem to break down a lot? Well, one answer could be that more parts come with new technology. More parts mean more potential problems. Another solution could be that they don't break down as much. It just may seem like they do because there are thousands more planes and flights. Another answer could be that the plane you're on now hasn't had a proper rest. A long time ago, an airplane would get a rest of 24 hours after a 4,000-mile journey. Not today. After 8,000 miles, it's cleaned, refueled, and off again, sometimes within an hour.

Can you imagine if you drove your car for ten hours straight, only to gas it up and go again?

It is true that a plane is built differently. It is designed to keep going, and when anything goes wrong with the engine, they either fix it or sometimes just replace it with a new engine. My thoughts are that it can't be that healthy to fly a plane 20 hours a day, seven days a week, 365 days a year, but that's what is happening on most airlines right now.

Think about inside the plane. Just imagine how much body perspiration the seat you're in has absorbed throughout this year. How many people have used the blanket around you before its last laundering? Yet, people will still walk around barefoot and let their children chew on the seat cushions.

It is rumored that a plane on the ground receives more damage than in the air flying. While that may be true, I would rather be on the ground when something did go wrong. I am not very confident on the overworking of an airplane that the flying industry is setting as standard. What I recommend to you as the passenger is to travel on the airlines with the younger fleets. (The information is provided at this website: *http://av-info.faa.gov/GetFleetAge.asp*) I once worked for an airline that skimped on maintenance measures and had the oldest planes around. I would never go back to those days again.

On one occasion, a piece of a wing fell off on the runway only to be taped back on with electrical tape, and the plane took off 30 minutes later. Things were broken outside as well as inside the plane, and were never fixed.

You can also tell a lot about an airline's maintenance department by the number of items broken inside the plane. People will tell you that it has no bearing on the maintenance outside the plane, but that is load of hooey. A poor maintenance department inside usually means a poor maintenance department outside.

These days, we are quite budget conscious, but before booking a ticket with that thrifty carrier, check and see just how much more a well known carrier costs. If it isn't much, don't you think it's worth your and your family's safety? If the ticket price is a lot less than all of the rest, then maybe you should ask yourself just what department is this particular airline skimping on?

Insecurity

WHILE I AM FAIRLY confident in my airline's safety measures, I am not so sure about airport security. Airline terrorism comes in and out of style, approximately every four years, and when it does, many people die. What surprises me most is that it doesn't occur more often.

In America, security measures are minimal, and it will take a catastrophe like TWA's flight #800 (even though the result was deemed non-terrorist activity) to bring heightened awareness to the threat of terrorism and the need for stricter security measures.

In Europe and some other foreign destinations, security is at maximum level and still probably not enough. We all know nothing is going to be 100 percent safe. There aren't as many plastic explosive detectors in America's airports as there should be, and only two out of four foreign airports possess them. Why? Because the cost is one million dollars and higher, per machine. The average passenger states that they wouldn't mind paying the extra cost involved if it was for security, but would probably moan and complain about the increased price nevertheless.

If the Federal Aviation Administration (FAA) got together and imposed a higher security tax on all flights there wouldn't be an option on where the money went. This way the airports could get up to speed on the very latest technology, even though terrorists will, unfortunately, get wiser as security gets tougher. I believe that at one time all successful terrorists must have worked at an airport. It filled me with horror when a colleague opened her bag in the middle of the flight to discover a box of chocolates or gift which had been put in there as a romantic gesture. Luckily, there are measures now to prevent that scenario from turning bad...but I could tell you many situations where there is nothing to prevent catastrophes from happening.

Not that this is something to be proud of, but I am pretty sure that I could penetrate the toughest of security sections. I would never try it on my own, but maybe after this book appears in bookstores, someone from the FAA will take me up on a challenge. Every time I go through a security check (which is all the time), I imagine ways of getting something by them. I have been cavity-searched in Bangkok, strip-searched in Moscow, had my shaving cream can destroyed in Japan, and had my personal diary read in South America. In the interest of security, I cooperated with all of these searches (not that I had a choice), yet I still saw ways of slipping by the toughest security checks. Maybe only a person with a deranged mind thinks of these things, but then again maybe it's a safety-conscious person, as well.

I believe that the National Transportation Safety Board (NTSB) could learn a lot from the flight crews. I even wrote a letter expressing my concerns about certain security, or lack of security, measures. I received a "thank you for your concern, but this is to inform you that we are operating at the highest level necessary blah blah blah" letter and felt like an idiot for writing it. If I can penetrate the toughest of security measures, just think about what someone with a twisted mind (more twisted, I mean) could do.

One aspect of higher security at airports is the questions you are asked by security personnel:

1. Have you had your hand luggage with you at all times?
2. Who packed your bags, and when?
3. Have you been asked to carry anything for anyone?
4. Do you have any battery-operated or electrical devices, or anything that looks like a weapon?

As you answer these questions, you're undoubtedly thinking to yourself, "If I was a terrorist, do you think I would tell the truth?" If you find these questions irrelevant, mundane, and rather a waste of time, remember this: Most bombs and weapons make it onto the airplanes in the luggage of innocent passengers. On Pan Am flight #103, the air disaster over Lockerbie, the bomb was concealed in a radio cassette player. These questions are asked primarily for your heightened awareness. So as you answer the questions the way you know is the correct way, deep in your mind you should be searching for the truthful answers. "Did I pack that bag? Did someone give me something to carry?"

Airlines and airports do have to toughen up their security, especially in the U.S.A. That point is pretty clear. Unfortunately, terrorism is now in style in the United States, and it looks like it's only getting worse. However, you as a passenger can do things to help as well:

1. Don't bitch and moan if you have to wait in a line at a security checkpoint longer than usual, or get too annoyed if you continue to set off the alarm of the metal detector.

2. Please complain if you witness a breach of security. For example, someone goes off in the metal detector and the security personnel miss them.

3. Report any baggage or unusual packages left unattended or any unusually suspicious-looking characters (although that would just about cover half of the airport).

4. Don't carry anything in your bag or on yourself for anyone, unless you're absolutely certain about the object. I would say never carry anything for anyone else, period, but we all know that we carry gifts and other items for family members.

5. Pack your own bags and keep them with you at all times until airline personnel take them from you.

6. Don't make a joke about security. It exists for your safety and mine. Bomb jokes are distasteful, dangerous, and against the law.

7. Ask questions when you don't understand an aspect of safety, or lack of safety. If you don't get a satisfactory answer, write to the FAA or NTSB. Maybe by then, they will be ready for fan mail reception.

Federal Aviation Administration
800 Independence Ave., SW
Washington, DC 20591
To report a safety violation, call the 24-Hour
Hotline at 800-255-1111
Website: *www.faa.gov*

National Transportation Safety Board
490 L'Enfant Plaza, SW
Washington, DC 20594
Phone: 202-314-6000
Website: *www.ntsb.gov*

I know many of you have other things on your mind when you travel, but take a few moments and think about the security around you. We spend enough time worrying about the worst that can happen; don't you think it's time we took an active role in doing something about it? The life you save may be your own, but it may be mine, as well.

The Bar is Closed

**"We reserve the right to refuse anyone alcohol,
as the flight attendants deem appropriate."**

PLEASE READ THIS STATEMENT and realize that it **is** our right! Believe me, it is for everyone's good, especially the person drinking. Nobody likes being told that they've had enough to drink, but when they make a scene about it, they look even worse. We don't count how many drinks you have had, because for all we know you could have chugged a liter in the departure lounge. We look for actions and reactions. Our main job up there is to look after your safety. Fifty percent of the danger comes from the other passengers around you. So we monitor that very closely, and if we say no more, then we mean no more. **Don't** beg, threaten to get us fired, go to a different cabin and ask, kick up a fuss, or fight it.

If we are wrong, then just accept it, and realize it's for the best and move on. We have the company's backing on this subject and, most importantly, we have the captain's backing, and we will have the plane met by the police, if necessary. I used to be a bartender and have extensive knowledge in this area, but have had my blunders as a F/A as well. Can you imagine my horror when I cut off a passenger, only to find out later that he wasn't drunk, but had muscular dystrophy?

A story that was recently in the headlines involved a flight from South America to New York. A passenger became so drunk that when he was cut off, he rebelled by going up to First Class, defecated on a service cart, and painted the walls with his feces.

When the plane landed, airline officials met him, along with the police, and later filed a lawsuit against him. He filed a claiming the airline was liable because they had served him too much alcohol.

He lost his lawsuit and was forced to reimburse the fares of all the passengers in the First Class cabin (approximately $100,000). He was also blacklisted from ever flying with that airline again. The shocker of the whole ordeal is that this guy was the CEO of a major company.

Can you imagine waking up the next morning and saying "I DID WHAT??!!!!"

I doubt that he is still with that company. I guess the shit really hit the fan. He gave a new meaning to the term "a shit flight."

The Summer of Air Discontent

YOU HAVE ALL READ in some of the previous chapters about how every flight is an opportunity for knowledge, adventure, and fun. Well, now I have to write about the other side of the coin. You, the passengers, my airline, the airline industry, my co-workers, and I went through possibly the worst summer of travel in a very long time, if not ever. The tragedies we all had to endure included weather, mechanically dysfunctional airplanes, overbooked flights, staff shortages, labor disputes, cancellations, management ignorance, and the list goes on. I saw staff and passengers react in ways I had never witnessed before. Many vacations were ruined. Passengers aboard airplanes were stuck out on runways for hours at a time. All summer long I worked on only one flight that left and returned on time without incident. If you flew in the summer of 2000, then you probably know what I mean.

Some airlines dealt with these problems better than others, but I am ashamed to say that mine did not. In fact, they reacted quite poorly. Even though I have limited liability in the way events played out that summer, I want to issue an extremely heartfelt apology. I am sorry for all you went through and hope that this doesn't deter you from future travel. If you had a bad experience with a certain airline, let them know in the form of a letter. If they don't offer some compensation, then go to another airline and try them on for size. Sometimes the only way to let them know you are dissatisfied is to hurt their profits. Sure, yelling at the flight attendant may feel good, but I can assure you that it does nothing.

I was on a five-hour coast-to-coast trip where the plane was dirty, there was no scheduled meal, no pillow or blankets were to be had, and we were three hours delayed. It didn't surprise me in the least, as my flight three days earlier was exactly the same. An elite member of our mileage program was on both of those flights. He yelled and lectured me for the majority of both flights about how this airline was so horrible to its customers. I really pissed him off when I agreed with him.

"Did you write a letter and complain?" I asked.
"No, I don't have time," he replied.
"Will you?"
"Probably not."
"Then I suggest trying another airline."
"No, I can't. I have too many miles in this mileage program."
"What possible good do you think yelling at me will do? You are unwilling to write a letter or switch airlines, and they will not listen to me," I firmly replied.
"Well, that sucks!"
"Yes, it does, sir. Yes, it sure does."

Folks, this is the way it is and will always be if you don't hit them where it hurts, the wallet. You are seeing some relief with the Passenger's Bill of Rights, but, believe me, the airlines will find ways out of that. If you don't like something, in the seat back pocket in front of you is an inflight magazine. There should be an address in the back to send complaints. Another equally good vehicle of complaint is filling out the surveys that come around from time to time. The Internet has lots of useful information on other airlines, route structure, and fares. If you're stuck in a mileage program, you can always join another. You won't lose the miles in the first one. I encourage you to voice your opinion, but I recommend the proper channels in order to be heard.

It's kind of comical that the "Summer 2000" fiasco came at a time when the big airlines had been trying to buy other airlines to increase their sizes. Don't you think that they should be able to handle the flights they already have before messing up any more flights? Just a crazy thought.

10

Grounded –
Tales and Tips

Deplane Truth

THE PROCESS OF DEPLANING can only be described as one big ugly mess. Get up in a hurry, grab your bags from the overhead bins, throw any and all trash on the ground, and wait for the slow line of people to get off. It's the old hurry up and wait without the manners. Most people are grumpy, tired, and probably not using caution when getting their bags from overhead. Then there is always that one passenger who puts his bags several rows back and insists on holding everyone up while retrieving them.

You have been in a metal cylindrical tube with wings for quite a few hours, enduring crying babies, loud neighbors, and uncomfortable seats. Now, it's time to get off.

If you want to save yourself a lot of stress and frustration, remain seated. Put on your headphones, listen to music, and watch. It's a ballet of characters and interesting acrobatics. People are naturally amusing, and the music adds a special touch to this comedy of life. It's like an ad lib performance of synchronized swimmers. Of course, everyone will look at you oddly while you laugh at them. Who cares? You'll probably never see them again, and you have saved yourself ten to twenty blood pressure points.

In line, most people end up waiting and complaining. You must also take into account that everyone getting up at once may produce an undesirable symphony of smells. The delays can get quite lengthy while you're standing next to the person that you have wanted to strangle the whole flight.

The wait becomes unbearable if the jetway breaks down or the airline doesn't catch your early or late arrival. It is then practically impossible to sit back down due to everyone and their bags in the aisle. The people who get up right away will, at most, beat you to the terminal by only a couple of minutes. The way I look at it, you've been in your seat for several hours. What are a few more minutes?

A Franc Lesson

MY LUCK IN PARIS has not been what one would call good. I have had a bad case of poison ivy, a severe case of food poisoning, and was a passenger in the worst car accident of my life. You'd think with my track record I would try to avoid that region of the world, but I can't. I love Paris and regard France as one of my favorite destinations. My wife speaks French. We fell in love in Bordeaux and have some of our fondest holiday memories from this country.

I was on a layover in Paris in the springtime and, although I was without my wife, I wanted to share it with some friends on the crew. After a full day of sightseeing I treated two of my female co-workers to a secret fondue place in the Montmartre district. We had stuffed ourselves with a delicious cheese feast and had indulged in far too much red wine. Although it was getting late, someone suggested we head to the Sacre-Coeur, which was a steep uphill half-mile away. We needed the exercise after that meal, anyway.

Almost to the top and out of breath, we had one last stretch of steps to go. All of a sudden one of my friends shrieked as two men walking down the steps grabbed her purse. One slit the purse strap with a knife and the other tugged it free. It all happened in an instant and before I knew it I was in a foot chase with two thugs. They saw me chasing so they split up at the bottom of the steps. I continued to chase the one with the purse tucked under his arm. Since it had started to rain lightly, the cobblestone had become quite slippery. I tripped a couple of times but luckily so did my assailant. Our chase continued through the back streets of Paris and across a few busy streets. I was actually catching up to him when we ran into a back alley. It was a dead end and he was cornered.

Now what, I thought to myself as the man slowly turned around and took out his knife. That was good enough for me. I turned to run away but was greeted by three of his friends.

"Take out your wallet and throw it to me," one of them shouted in a broken French accent.

"Can't we talk about this, guys?" I implored in a desperate effort to end the situation peacefully.

One of them smirked, "He wants to talk?" They continued to walk toward me. I felt a blow to the back of my head, as the fellow behind me apparently hit me with the butt of his knife. I woke up in a hospital bed with the mother of all headaches and feeling sore from head to toe. But I was lucky to be alive!

From this experience I learned many valuable lessons that I would like to pass on to you.

1. When traveling, always bring a dummy purse or wallet. Put only the bare essentials in it: one credit card, one piece of photo identification, and enough cash for the intended outing. Leave everything else in the hotel. If you insist on bringing it all with you, purchase a safety-carrying pouch that straps to your body. The woman's purse that was stolen was a dummy purse and had no valuables in it; unfortunately, my wallet had everything in it.

2. Men: Always keep your wallet in your front pocket. Women: Slip your purse over your shoulder with the strap coming down diagonally across your torso, with the purse opening facing inward against your body.

3. If you encounter someone trying to take your purse or wallet, yell loudly. The attention from others hearing your yell will possibly scare them away.

4. Don't fight your assailants. If you struggle too hard you might get seriously hurt. Remember, someone who cuts your purse strap could cut you just as easily.

5. Don't be a hero. I learned the hard way. Being the only male in my group, I felt that it was my duty to catch them. Besides being almost hit by two cars, beaten up, and my wallet taken, I could have been killed.

6. If someone threatens you and demands your wallet or purse, just give it to them. Don't get cute or refuse. It is just a leather contraption that holds your personal items. Your life isn't as replaceable.

7. Don't assume a person lying on the side of a back street is homeless. Apparently, the French lady who found me mistook me for a vagrant – which is understandable since I was passed out, reeking of booze from the wine I'd had earlier, and my clothes were all messed up. Call the police or alert someone in the vicinity.

8. Trust your gut instincts. I wasn't too happy about being out sightseeing so late at night, but shrugged it off as being overprotective and went along with the consensus, without voicing my opposition.

This advice should be utilized in any major city. Crime is a fact of life everywhere, and your awareness and safety precautions are your number one defense.

My wife and I are planning a trip next month to France starting off with a weekend in Paris. I am a bit weary but look forward to getting back on the horse, as they say. Hopefully, I can break my string of bad luck. First stop, fondue!

Let's Do the Bump

AIRLINES ARE IN BUSINESS to get you comfortably and safely from one place to another. But let's face it, they're in it primarily for the money. That's why, sometimes when you show up for your flight, they ask for volunteers to take a later flight. It's called a bump, and it usually includes bribes of upgrades and money.

Why do the airlines oversell flights? Because passengers have an average no-show rate of approximately 15%. If they booked 300 passengers for a flight with 300 seats to Europe, on average 45 people would not show up. The airplane would still go to Europe but with 45 empty seats. The passengers who don't show get their money back, but the airline loses the revenue of those 45 seats. In a sense, the airline is depending on the passenger to be 15% unreliable; it's when everybody shows up that it starts getting interesting.

It can be a very annoying and frustrating aspect of flying, but let's discuss a different aspect of the bump. I met a passenger one late August afternoon waiting for the same flight as I was. Unfortunately, the flight was full, and I was not going to get on.

A pass rider (an employee on standby) knows he is in trouble when an announcement is made, asking for volunteers from revenue passengers to take another flight. The offer usually includes an upgrade on the next flight, a $400 flight coupon good for any travel, and, if needed, hotel accommodations. If they don't get enough volunteers the price goes up. I have seen the price go up to $1,200 and a First Class ticket on any flight on our airline. People usually scoff at the announcement, because they've got to be where they've got to be, and when they've got to be there.

A certain passenger – I'll call him Smart Stanley – had a smile on his face and was quite pleased as the price for volunteers went up.

"Why are you so pleased?" I inquired.

"Well, as the offer goes up, so does my price," he chuckled back.

"I don't follow you."

"Well, I volunteered right away, and even though I volunteered at a lower price, as the lack of volunteers rises, so does the offer, and so does my price."

I talked to him further, even though I should have been finding alternate flight and accommodation plans. He told me that he had been there three days in a row, and volunteered to be bumped off of every one of them.

He had raked in $3,100 worth of flight coupons, three nights in a lovely hotel in a great city, free meal vouchers, four free 15-minute long-distance phone calls, and an upgrade on the next flight he gets on (if he gets on). He said it happened every year, and that this was his third year in a row that he did "the bump thing" as he put it.

He ran his own business and planned his vacation for the same time and same flight every year. While he did have plans when he finally arrived, he collected his business's travel money for the year doing that "bump thing."

He said that you would have thought the airline would catch on by now, but they don't care – just as long as they get a volunteer, they're happy. One year he collected over $8,000 and ended up getting a refund on his ticket after a week and a half of being bumped. Another smart thing he did was choose a flight that left only once a day; that way he got his nightly stays.

Stanley said last year was a bad year, because he only got bumped twice, but he had a wonderful vacation and got bumped on the way back. He knew that I was a pass rider, so he offered me a place to sleep that night. Considering that there wasn't going to be a vacant room in the city, I took him up on it. He had bet the manager of the hotel that he would be back, and obviously won, so he got a suite (comparable to two rooms in one).

We ate and drank on the airline's meal voucher and tried the next day. Well, when the same announcement was made the next day, Stanley started to chuckle again, and I bade him farewell. I had to scramble for a way to get back to work, and the other flights weren't looking very promising. I never saw him again, but am sure that if I

went to that flight at the end of August, he'd be on the list for that "bump thing."

Now, I am not recommending that you do what Stanley did, or probably still does, but if you do hear that announcement and can afford the time, go for it. There are lots of rewards in it. Who knows, it could be an adventure.

The time of year that bumping most often occurs is over most major holidays, spring break, and the beginning and end of summer. Stanley recommends August 29 through September 7. It usually happens when there are only one or two flights a day to a specific destination. Don't worry if the price of the bump goes up and you have already settled on a lower price. The highest offer is always good for all accepted volunteers.

Make sure, if you are offered an upgrade for the next flight, to take it. If it is not available when the next flight rolls around, make sure you get some kind of compensation. Otherwise, refuse, stating that you were promised an upgrade. Get what they offer in writing and write down the name of the agent and his or her ID number. If you don't, you have no proof of the offer. If you receive a ticket as a bumper reward, remember that if you get offered another bump at that time, take it and make them pay!

Happy Bumping!

Forty Winks Away
From Home

HOTELS HOLD A VERY special place in every F/A's heart. They are the places we rest our heads after a long day's work. They're the haven where we hide away from other people who may have a request or drink order. Most F/As will encounter at least one hotel every time they go to work.

F/As have odd hotel hours. We might check in at 2 a.m. and check out at 10 p.m., so getting proper sleep may be a challenge. For example, at 8 a.m. the attack of the morning staff begins. The housekeeping army is on the full offensive, and I do mean fully offensive. The whining and banging of vacuums, slamming of doors, and the yelling of instructions to one another are enough to drive you crazy. In Europe, I have been awakened many times by hotel staff checking for a depleted mini-bar. Can you imagine waking up to some strange man at the foot of your bed counting drinks? The "Do Not Disturb" sign may be on the door, but he seems to have immunity.

I value sleep immensely, so through the years I have gathered some tricks to the art of sleeping away from home. The following is a list of tips for a happier hotel sleep:

1. **Earplugs** – It's very important that you get used to wearing them. Put them by the bedside table. Bring a back-up pair, just in case.

2. **Room choice** – Don't get a room by the elevator or ice machine. You will feel the vibration all night long. It may

not be apparent at first, but, believe me, when the lights are out, it will be. One more thing: if the hotel has a disco, make sure you get a room at least two floors away. I can't tell you how many nights in South America I tried to sleep to the beat.

3. **Do Not Disturb sign** – If your room does not have one, call the concierge, and do not fall asleep until they bring you one. Without it, housekeeping will drive you bananas in the morning. The amount of times the maid has caught me in a naked stumble for my bathroom visit is shocking.

4. **Operator** – Call the operator and ask for a "do not disturb" on your phone line. Wrong-number calls will abound and are apt to ruin your slumber. You can request a "do not disturb" until a certain time or until you call and cancel.

5. **Party time** – If there is a party going on next door, do not, and I repeat, do not call security on the assumption they will solve the matter. Instead, I recommend packing your bags, returning to the front desk, and requesting another room. It's very easy for the front desk to say that they have no more rooms on the phone, but much more difficult to say it in person. If you feel unduly inconvenienced by the partyers, you could always remember their room number and then give them a call early the next morning. They are bound to be in mid-sleep with a hangover waiting. The same goes for the loud couple next door going for the sexual marathon record. It's fun to listen to for the first ten minutes but will make you cringe when it goes on for hours.

6. **Television timer** – If there is a timer function on the remote control, set it no matter how awake you feel. Waking up to a horror or war movie on high volume is a scary experience.

7. **Trailblazing** – Make a clear path from the bed to the toilet. This is so you don't have to turn a light on or stub a toe on the way to your nightly visit.

8. **Liquids** – Keep a glass or, better yet, a bottle of water within hand reach. Looking for some in the middle of the night might ruin any chance of getting back to sleep.

9. **Curtains** – Close the curtains so the sun doesn't wake you in the morning.

10. **Alarming** – Check to be sure that the alarm clock has been turned off. There are F/As who get a kick out of setting it for the middle of the night as a practical joke for the next guest. Not my type of humor, but it's out there.

I know the list may sound long and a bit of a hassle, but when you value sleep as much as I do, it is well worth it. Sweet dreams!

Check Please

"OUT OF ALL THE places in the world, which is your favorite place to go?"

"What's your favorite city?"

"Which country is your favorite?"

"Where was your best vacation?"

These are all similar questions, but at the same time they are very different, each one returning a different answer. I get asked these questions all the time, but unfortunately there is never a standard answer. It's true I have been all over the world, but it's the circumstances that make the experiences, as well as the place. It's whom you're with, things that happen, weather, lucky breaks, activities, etc.

Therefore, my honest answer would be that I like different places for different reasons. It is a bit of a cop-out, I realize, but if I had to state a specific place it would have to be Prague, Czech Republic.

My girlfriend and I arrived in Frankfurt for the connecting flight to Africa, only to discover that it was canceled due to the terrorist threats and actions in some of the neighboring African regions. It was supposed to remain closed for the next two weeks. We had planned a two-week safari in Kenya, so that trip was a washout.

We were all packed, but had nowhere to go. We were at a loss on what to do next. We decided to drop a pen on the European section of the map and wherever it landed would be the place we would go. It landed on Prague.

"Where's Prague? Isn't it Communist? Are we allowed to go there?" It was in early 1990, shortly after the Revolution. There was little information available, but we found out that we were allowed in without a visa.

I voted for dropping the pen again, but she disagreed. We looked at the monitor and saw that a plane for Prague was leaving in one hour. We decided to go for it. We hooked up on the plane with a few female students who were going there the same as us, "clueless."

The trip turned out to be spectacular. It was a beautiful city, rich with culture, preserved history, dirt-cheap prices and, best of all, not many tourists. Although hotels were scarce, many locals were renting out their houses. We rented a house in the middle of town with the three students, and it came to a whopping $20 per day for all of us combined. It was one of those spur-of-the-moment decisions that really paid off.

It was a country unaffected by commercialism, untouched by war, and, my God, those prices were unbelievable! A seven-course meal for a dollar, a huge pint of their delicious beer was 12 cents (no, not a mistype – twelve cents). Everything was cheap, history was rich, the locals were friendly, Prague was beautiful, and everywhere we went, people were celebrating the end of the Revolution.

I am fairly certain, however, that it won't be that way now. I wouldn't want to go back and tarnish my wonderful memories. In addition, I have heard the stories of the commercialism that has taken place, such as a McDonald's at every corner and the tourism trade taking its toll, although I am sure it would still be a fun getaway. Some of the most unlikely places can be the best getaways. I would say Prague was that place for me.

Carrying On

ALL RIGHT, FOLKS, WHAT is the deal with this hand luggage epidemic we're having? It's a disease and it's growing like wildfire. Airlines have invested billions of dollars in automated baggage systems in order to relieve the burden of carrying your luggage around, yet more and more of you are deciding not to take that chance.

The average airline loses a reported four out of 10,000 bags. Those are monumental odds. I have flown for over 13 years and never (knock on wood) had my bag lost. It's true that I don't check my bag when I am working, but I do when I am on vacation or off time (and believe me, with free travel, that's a lot). What you should do, if you're worried, is have your carry-on bag contain your valuables, passports, personals, and maybe a change of clothes. Airlines usually compensate up to $1,400 (different for each airline) for each lost bag. If it does disappear, you'll get a new wardrobe and some spending money.

OK, putting the odds aside, don't you find it a relief to say goodbye to your bags and then stroll around the airport free of any excess weight? If only we could check our kids.... You want to enjoy your experience, not worry about lugging your bags around. If you are an experienced traveler, then maybe you don't want to enjoy it, but you probably want to minimize the aggravation involved.

I remember a certain passenger who had four bags disguised as two. He had his computer, printer, VCR, and all of his clothes carefully packed away. He got them by the ticket counter by hiding them behind the desk. He got them by the security checkpoints, but every one of his bags was searched. He even got them by the check-in agents, but when he got to the plane the F/A took one look at him and said "No way!" He argued with the F/A for about 20 minutes, then gave in (he had no choice). So he had struggled for two hours in vain, his blood pressure probably raised ten or more points, and he was ready to thoroughly hate the ten-hour flight. It is a stress not worth going through.

Don't check the following items:

1. Heart or any other necessary medication.
2. Passports, tickets, checks, credit cards, and currency.
3. Phone numbers and other important papers.
4. Jewelry and priceless heirlooms.
5. Fragile items.
6. Weapons or items shaped as weapons (don't bring them at all, or ask the airline for specific instructions).

It's not the stress of carrying your bags that is the main point in all of this. Carry-on luggage can fall from an overhead container if packed too tightly or is too heavy. It can be left places, causing fear of a bomb threat. It also causes delays finding safe storage space. Most airlines are trying to crack down on this issue, but it can be tough, especially with travel guides and tips advising you to try avoiding the check-in bag procedure.

FACT: Most bags reported lost are those that get checked in at the last moment; i.e., when you have your bag taken off at the gate because it's too big, it might miss its connection because it is not properly tagged. Then you blame me, because I took it from you. Yes, there was plenty of room in the First Class closet, but we can't put all 400 oversized bags in there.

If you have ever wondered why those lazy F/As don't come rushing toward you to help you with your carry-on luggage, think of this: the average domestic F/A's day consists of six flights, with six boardings, take-offs, and landings. Each flight brings a new set of passengers, with new sets of bags carrying prospective kitchen sinks. It is their duty to find a safe and legal stowage area for every piece of carry-on luggage.

What you don't know is that if F/As throw their backs out while specifically lifting your carry-on bags, they are not covered by the company's insurance policy. Not only are the F/As irritated with the amount of luggage allowed in the cabin, but they're also neither stupid nor looking for that back sprain. So, take heed, all future plumbers and sink carriers, we're not gonna stow it for you. They may do that on foreign airlines, but not on American carriers.

Now on to a subject that may be the most frightening aspect of check-in luggage – your pets. We all hear of the tragedies of pets dying in the hold or getting loose and never being found again. These are extremely rare occurrences and should not be cause for alarm. Your pets are very safe in the cargo hold. All compartments are cabin pressurized and the temperature is monitored just as it is in the cabin. They might be a bit frightened and angry by the time you see them again, but you would be, too, if you were in a dark room with many movements and weird sounds and forced to sleep in your own feces. If you like your pet, you will get a doggie-downer from your veterinarian, which will knock your pet out for a while and will minimize the shock.

Once in a while I work on a plane with a downstairs kitchen, and I hear the dogs barking. Yes, I feel sorry for them a bit, but I know that they will be okay. If you have a question about pet transport, call your specific airline for instructions. Also, ask about quarantine laws that apply for specific countries.

Jacket and Thai Required

I HAD MANAGED THE impossible: three weeks off in July, and I had even managed to get on a flight to Bangkok, using a "space available" ticket. I had never been to Thailand before, but I knew from all the stories that I was in for an adventure. I was on a different airline than the one I worked for, so I had to be on my best behavior. I limited myself to a couple of beers, and a meal of disappointingly half-cooked chicken curry. I was hungry, so I ate it anyway.

A favorite flying pastime for F/As is comparing services of a different airline with their own. I was expecting much more from this one, especially because they claimed to be the people's favorite airline. It wasn't my favorite, but then again I was paying $75 to go 5,000 miles. Who was I to complain?

My friends were supposed to meet me there in a few days. I never expected to get on a flight on my first try, especially in July. This meant that I would have a few days to discover Bangkok on my own. There were plenty of hostels and cheap hotels around the city so I wasn't unduly worried. I fell asleep with excitement and adventure fresh in my mind. I woke up four hours later with the harshest of headaches. Sweat streamed off my forehead and multiple knots churned in my stomach. Saliva raced to my mouth. I was about to throw up, and if I wasn't quick enough, my neighbor was going to get doused. I spent the remainder of the flight throwing up every particle in my stomach in 30-minute intervals.

I wished I were dead. I even prayed for God to take me right then and there. No such luck. I fell asleep actually hugging the toilet. I awoke to the sound of the captain announcing our initial descent into Bangkok, and stumbled back to my seat feeling weak, but pretending to be all right. I filled out the landing card, necessary for customs and immigration. It had a skull and cross bones next to the statement "DRUG TRAFFICKERS WILL BE EXECUTED!"

I had my gear together but couldn't find my right shoe. Everyone deplaned as I searched in vain for it. A F/A helped me for a while, but it was nowhere to be seen. I limped off the airplane, feeling weak and deathly ill, my hair defying gravity, two black eyes from the burst blood vessels, with one shoe, and on my first time to Thailand.

I went to the immigration desk and the first question out of the man's mouth was, "Why you look sick?" He did not mince words.

"Something I ate on the plane, I guess."

I don't think he liked my response. "Where your shoe?"

"I don't know," I said, getting a little bit annoyed, and starting to feel sick again.

I was sent directly to secondary screening. I entered a small dark room with a man sitting in a chair, eating an apple.

"Take off your shirt and empty your pockets," he said, not taking his eyes off his apple.

I started to get scared, so I complied 100 percent. My pockets were jammed full of tissues just in case I got sick. His eyes widened at this and ordered me to take off my pants. As I did this, a man entered with my suitcase and threw it on the floor. The contents had obviously been searched, emptied, and stuffed unceremoniously back in.

"Now take rest off."

"Wait a minute, what's going on here?" I replied.

"Do it, or you find trouble." He threw his apple in the nearby trash.

That was a good enough response to me. I removed my underwear and socks. I was instructed to turn around and to spread my butt cheeks apart. I was able to do this, but got sick again all over my underwear beside me.

"What kind of drugs you on?"

"I told you, it's food poisoning. I'm not on any drugs." I felt like crying.

He told me to get dressed, and then continued to interrogate me to find out the names and flight numbers of my friends who were arriving in three days time. I didn't question why; I just did it. I blew my budget and headed for the nearest expensive hotel, where I lay in bed for the next 72 hours.

I had almost recovered by the time my friends arrived. They were two hours late, due, they said, to some kind of stupid secondary screening that they had to go through. I acted surprised and kept my mouth shut.

Initial Descent

"FOURTEEN ONE-THOUSAND, FIFTEEN one-thousand, breathe."
I repeated to myself as I knelt over a 300-pound collapsed man. It
was difficult enough finding out where his chest started and stomach
began, much less finding the heart to try to revive life into this poor
man.

He was an elderly gentleman and smelt as if he had been bathing
in Scotch while smoking a whole pack of cigarettes. I cringed every
time I had to breathe for him. I remember this man's last comment
to me was how bad the airline was, and what a pathetic job we were
doing. Regardless, I willed life through his veins with every compres-
sion. Nobody had volunteered to help when we made an announcement requesting a doctor on board; therefore, I went ahead. I hoped
and prayed that I was doing everything right, with knowledge of only
basic airline-taught CPR.

After a few minutes, which seemed like hours of compressions, I
felt for a heartbeat and found one this time. This man was back in
the land of the living. It had worked. All the training that I had
ridiculed and demeaned had actually paid off. A doctor finally came
forward, cautiously at first, and only once he realized that the patient
was alive. I relinquished my position to the doctor.

I sat back on the floor of the aisle, dripping in sweat, and watched
the doctor take care of the patient. I was in awe of the fact that only
a few minutes ago this man had no heartbeat and was in all senses
dead. I was quite proud of myself. It was the first time in a long while
that I could say that I had made a difference in someone's life, apart
from quenching thirst and satisfying hunger.

A passenger leaned over to me for what I thought was going to be
a "Good job" or "Way to go." He looked around, cupped his hand to

his mouth, and whispered, "Hey, buddy, can I get a diet coke?"

I merely laughed as reality set back in. When we landed, they took the sick man away in an ambulance. A couple of months later, I received a thank you letter and a picture of him with his three grandchildren. It was a beautiful picture, aside from the burning cigarette in his left hand.

The airline also sent me a beautiful thank you note, disguised as a lawsuit disclaimer form. It touched me.

Oh, yeah, by the way, the man in 30B got his diet coke.

Making the Most of Your Trip

I'M NOT GOING TO tell you how to enjoy your trip when you're there. Different people have different forms of entertainment. One person might like the museums of Amsterdam, while another prefers the red light district. Different strokes for different folks.

I can only offer a few tips that might enhance your stay while you're there.

1. Stay away from room service whenever possible. It's costly, anti-social, and anti-cultural.

2. Stay away from fast food conveniences. Just about everywhere in this world is McDonald's. Go to an authentic local restaurant; you can have a Big Mac at home.

3. Variety is the spice of life, and it should be abroad, as well. If you're there for the museums, it doesn't mean you can't explore the other aspects of the country you're in. Go to Chinatown or the local open-air market for a taste of something different.

4. Try to learn a little of the country's language. Even if everyone understands English, the locals generally appreciate the effort.

5. Try to blend in a bit. Don't broadcast the fact that you're a tourist. Dress in a similar fashion as everyone else. For example, don't wear *lederhosen* (suspenders) in Bavaria

when no one else does, except for special occasions. You might offend someone, plus you'll look like a fool. You won't get hassled as much if your attire doesn't scream "foreigner," and it's a lot safer.

6. If you enjoy a drink or two, go to a local tavern and have a tipple with the natives. Ask the hotel concierge where the more reputable ones are.

7. Be safety conscious, but don't think that everyone is out to rip you off.

8. Be adventurous and flexible; some of the best experiences are unplanned or unexpected.

9. Try to look at the positive aspects of your trip, rather than dwelling on the negative.

10. Take a chance! How many times are you going to go there in your lifetime?

See You Next Time...

I HAD A TOUGH time selecting a title for this book, because I had so many options.

Here's a few:

1. The Flight Less Traveled
2. Glamour in a Sick Bag.
3. Hey, Sit the Hell Down!
4. I Went to College for This?
5. The View From Up There.
6. Coffee, Tea, or You Know the Deal.
7. Marry Me, Fly Almost Free.
8. Observations from 35,000 Feet.
9. Confessions of a Flight Attendant
10. Everything You Always Wanted to Know About Commercial Flying, and Some You Didn't.

Thanks for flying with me. I hope you have enjoyed your flight. See you next time.

Buh Bye!!!!

In-Flight Dictionary

IF YOU HAVE EVER heard two F/As speaking to one another, you could be convinced that they are speaking another language. Every job has its own terminology; this is a look into ours. It is important to explain that while I poke fun with some terms, most, if not all, are truly used as everyday airplane vocabulary.

Aft: A term meaning the rear of the airplane.

Argumentative: A real pain in the ass.

Appears to be intoxicated: Drunk.

ATC: Air Traffic Control

Bidlines: A flight attendant's compilation of the next month's flying.

Bladder bags: A passenger who wants three drinks at a time and has to go to the restroom only when the meal carts are in the aisle.

Block in: The plane arrives at the gate.

Block out: The plane pushes back from the gate.

Briefing: A flight attendant meeting before a flight to discuss the working positions, special circumstances, times, and any other information pertaining to that particular flight.

Bulkhead: No, not some big head blocking the movie screen. The wall partition separating the cabins.

Captain: The pilot who is in command of the flight. The final word. If he comes to the cabin to solve a passenger problem, you know it's serious.

Contract: A small book that F/As carry to remind them of their rights in certain circumstances.

Credenza: A fixed table, usually located in First Class

Crew rest area: The area that is curtained off from the passengers for the crew to rest. If the curtains are closed we would appreciate it if you would not make a lot of noise around that area or peek in.

Crop dusting: The method that a F/A or passenger uses to dispel gas (fart) as they are walking up the aisles.

Church key: A soda can opener, there to spare the females finger nails.

Deadhead: A paid crew member sitting as a passenger. Usually a F/A or pilot on an irregular operation. They are allowed to sleep, dress, and drink like a normal passenger (oh, dear).

Decaf: Watered down regular coffee.

Decompression: Loss of cabin pressure. Usually associated with a loud bang, misty air, and oxygen masks dropping in front of your face. A word to the wise: if you see a mask, grab it and use it.

Deferred: The mechanics can't fix it either.

ETA: Estimated time of arrival.

FAA: Federal Aviation Administration. They govern the airlines.

F/A: Flight Attendant.

F/O: First Officer. Usually a pilot or a polite way of saying F@$& Off.

Froo froo: The elaborate linen folds found in First or in Business Class.

Galley: The kitchen or service area.

Ghost rider: One who is paid to act like a passenger, but is actually there to spy on the F/As and the service.

I.B.S. : In-flight briefing sheet. The sheet that explains all the details of the flight.

I.D.: The flight pattern identification number that the F/A or F/O can reference when specifying a certain trip.

Inop: Broken, out of order, kaput.

Jetway: The long cylindrical ramp that connects the airplane with the airport terminal. It's also the thing that breaks down 50 percent of the time.

Jumpseat: Crew seat for take-off and landing.

Jumpseater: Crew member who flies in uniform, when off duty, for free.

Lavatory: The toilet or restroom. The 2-1/2 ft. by 2-1/2 ft cubicle to do the necessities. But known throughout this book and to airline crews as the lav.

Legality: F/A or pilot term for how long they can be on duty before walking out on a flight (presumably still on the ground).

Manifest: The sheet of paper that the ground crew hands to the Chief F/A right before pushback. It states the final count and the specifics of each passenger. It can have special information like disabled, connecting flights, flight problems, frequent flyers, scared to fly, etc. I have even seen "This guy is a real pain in the ass." (He was, too.)

Manual check: A F/A's unauthorized break.

Mechanical: Something is wrong with the plane.

Misappropriated: Dropped on the floor.

Narrator: A pilot who makes long monotonous announcements.

On board supervisor: A supervisor who is on board to check the service flow and that proper procedures are being implemented. There won't be any fun or shortcuts on that flight.

Passrider: An airline worker on a free ticket. See **S/A**.

Pax: Short for passenger.

People mover: A bus that attaches to the airplane and takes passengers to either Customs or to the airport gates.

Pre-boarding: The time set aside for families with small children, or persons with disabilities needing extra help boarding the aircraft.

Pre-departure: The champagne or orange juice that is served before take-off.

Probation: New F/A on the first six months of flying.

Purser: F/A who is in charge of the flight service.

Pushback: The airplane pushes away from the gate.

Queen carts: The open-framed carts used in First and Business Class.

Remote gate: A gate nowhere near the airport terminal. Most likely it means a bus to or from the plane.

Reserve: A F/A who is on call to fly whenever the airline is short of crew for a particular flight.

Rolling delay: When they say there will be an hour delay, and come back in an hour and say another hour, and so on.

S/A: Space available. Usually an airline company employee whose ticket is free or cheap, who only gets a seat if there is one not taken at the end of boarding.

Satellite: Running meals or drinks by hand.

Standby: Same thing but includes normal passengers as well.

Slam click: A F/A who doesn't go out on the layovers.

Slot-time: The time scheduled with ATC to take off. If the plane misses that, it could be several hours before you get another one.

S.O.P.: Standard operating procedure.

Steward or stewardess: Old fashioned and out of date. The correct term is flight attendant.

Understaffed: A flight lacking enough F/As. Usually resulting in a diminished service.

U.M.: Unaccompanied minor.

Wanna-Be: a passenger who gets upgraded to First or Business Class and expects the world.

Water-landing: Also known as a ditching to crew members. Not a good sign.

Wheelies: The attachable wheels that fit onto suitcases, saving the back from strain.

CALL

BESIDES BARTENDER, WAITER, jazz trumpet player in Germany, interpreter, freelance writer, Frank Steward has worked as a flight attendant with two major international carriers during the past twelve years. He has flown over five million miles, encountered over half a million passengers, endured over a thousand different delays and cancellations, argued with over five hundred frequent flyers, flown to approximately a hundred countries, probably offended over a dozen cultures, and has more than a few pieces of advice and stories to pass on to the traveling public. He lives in the U.S. with his wife Martha, where they both work as flight attendants for a major international carrier.

Frank provides you with a new outlook on flying. If anyone should know, a frank steward should.

Be Frank!!